around

NEW YORK CITY
with KIDS

by Samantha Chapnick

5th EDITION
FODOR'S TRAVEL PUBLICATIONS
New York * Toronto * London * Sydney * Auckland
www.fodors.com

Credits
Writer: Samantha Chapnick

Editor: Maria Teresa Hart
Editorial Production: Evangelos Vasilakis
Production Manager: Steve Slawsky

Design: Fabrizio La Rocca, *creative director*
Cover Art and Design: Jessie Hartland
Flip Art and Illustration: Rico Lins, Keren Ora Adomoni/
Rico Lins Studio

About the Writer

Samantha Chapnick is a travel journalist and digital content expert. Founder of the Nickelodeon Best Blog in New York City (Parents Connect award winner) and kidcityny.com, she's also the NY Family Travel Expert for Examiner.com. Her writing has appeared in ForbesTraveler.com, Robb Report, New York Family, Rough Guides, and Frommer's. She has been recommended by *Travel and Leisure* and *Conde Nast Traveler* magazine.

Fodor's Around New York City with Kids

Fifth Edition
ISBN 978-1-4000-0515-4
ISSN 1526-1468

An Important Tip and an Invitation

Although all prices, opening times, and other details in this book are based on information supplied to us as of this writing, changes occur all the time in the travel world, and Fodor's cannot accept responsibility for facts that become outdated or for inadvertent errors or omissions. So always confirm information when it matters, especially if you're making a detour to visit a specific place. Your experiences—positive and negative—matter to us. If we have missed or misstated something, please write to us. We follow up on all suggestions. Contact the Around New York City with Kids editor at editors@fodors.com or c/o Fodor's at 1745 Broadway, New York, New York 10019.

Special Sales

This book is available for special discounts for bulk purchases for sales promotions or premiums. Special editions, including personalized covers, excerpts of existing books, and corporate imprints, can be created in large quantities for special needs. For more information, write to Special Markets/Premium Sales, 1745 Broadway, MD 6-2, New York, New York 10019, or e-mail specialmarkets@randomhouse.com.

PRINTED IN THE UNITED STATES OF AMERICA
10 9 8 7 6 5 4 3 2 1

COUNTDOWN TO GOOD TIMES

GET READY, GET SET!

New York City might be a huge metropolis of museums, shows, elegant dinners, and historic sites to you. But not to your kids (unless they've recently waxed poetic about the subtleties in Rothko's *Untitled* or requested more frisée in their salads).

Picture NYC from a kid's perspective and a different city materializes. One filled with fountains to splash in, toy stores to raid, Alice in Wonderland-like statues to climb, 40+ flavor ice-cream parlors to savor, exotic animals to meet, and lights and heights to marvel at.

A vacation is supposed to be more stimulating and less stressful than everyday life. With some advance planning, realistic expectations, and creative juggling your time in New York will surpass all expectations.

LOOK INSIDE

This book does more than give you ideas on places to go. It makes your trip a welcome break, as a vacation should be. Each two-page spread in this book describes a great place to take your family. The "toolbar" at the top of the page lists all the particulars: address, phone number, Web sites, admission prices, hours, and age recommendations. For each attraction we've also included boxes that include travel tips (**Keep in Mind**), time-savers (**Make the Most of Your Time**), and suggestions for kid-friendly dining (**Eats for Kids**) that can help you structure your visit.

Here are some overall hints covering most places and experiences you'll have in the Big Apple.

AVOID THE CROWDS

The most crowded times to do anything tourist-focused (e.g., Empire State Building) are, from most crowded to least, major holidays, weekends, and afternoons. Attractions popular for school field trips (e.g., the American Museum of Natural History) are busiest weekdays until around 2 pm. Surprisingly, the ideal times to do local hotspots, neighborhood strolls, and shopping (the latest restaurants, insider events) are weekends, especially long holiday weekends like July 4th when residents have fled to their beach or country houses. Overall, Sunday until noon, when all the city's singletons are still sleeping off Saturday's parties, is the city's most tranquil moment.

RECIPROCAL MEMBERSHIPS/CORPORATE SPONSORS

The easiest way to save money on your city trip is through free admission to popular museums and other not-for-profit institutions. Often museums have one night per week or per month when you can get in for free. If that does not work with your schedule, most have reciprocal membership agreements with other US institutions. If you are a member at a certain level (typically somewhere around $150 and above) of your local art or children's museum, science center, or zoo, all you need do is show your membership card to gain free admission to a sister institution here. For example, the New York Hall of Science is part of a network of 321 other attractions. Alternatively, if you work for a corporation that is a sponsor of an institution, you can often get in for free by showing your company ID. Finally, members of AAA and the military, seniors, and students should always ask whether there is a reduced or free admission policy. In many cases we've listed reduced admission in our pages.

SOCIAL MEDIA SPECIALS

Many organizations, including hotels, restaurants, and theaters, offer discounts, special amenities, or freebies through social media. Facebook friends and Twitter followers often get special deals like percentage-off hotel rates, discount theater tickets, or at the very least up-to-the-minute info on what's happening. It pays to look up NYC's attractions before you visit.

Another way to snag incredible discounts is to subscribe to local daily deal e-mails. Web sites like groupon.com send an offer you must buy within 24 hours, which can then be used for up to a year or longer. Typical offers include discounted restaurant meals, half-off museum memberships, or a month of yoga classes for the price of a week. The best sites include Groupon, BloomSpot, and Living Social.

PRIX-FIXE SAVERS

Many restaurants, from your corner Chinese joint to your celebrity-chef venue, do a prix-fixe limited lunch menu including an appetizer and entrée with seating in a more casual space (the bar or a special café area) and relatively quick service (less than 45 minutes total time). This is perfect for gourmand families wanting to eat at New York's finest in an economical, relatively kid-friendly way or those wanting to find the absolute best in cheap eats.

WELL KIDS = WONDERFUL KIDS

Although it would be easier to put in eateries catering purely to kids' tastes, many of the meals they love have more high-fructose corn syrup than a bag of Halloween candy. While we have included places to get "treats" (what's a vacation without some ice cream?), wherever possible we've suggested healthy meals.

DON'T FORGET TO WRITE

Is there a special attraction in our countdown that your family especially enjoys? Did we overlook one of your favorite places? We'd love to hear from you. Send your e-mails to me c/o editors@fodors.com. Please include "Around New York City with Kids" in the subject line. Or drop me a line by snail mail c/o Around New York City with Kids, Fodor's Travel Publications, 1745 Broadway, New York, NY 10019.

Happy traveling!

—Samantha Chapnick

ALLEY POND ENVIRONMENTAL CENTER

68

Brace yourself. Kids lacking a mini-zoo at home will be begging you for at least one pet upon departure. Lucky for you, the gift shop doesn't sell anything live.

For nature- and animal-loving kids, an excursion to this environmental center in Queens is well worth the travel time, thanks to its placement (secreted next to a major freeway, yet a world away) and its price (free!).

The Alley Pond Environmental Center is two facilities. One is an indoor building with classrooms, a party area, a gift shop, two aquarium tanks, and—most relevant to kids—a room with plenty of small mammals and reptiles. The other is the surrounding grounds, which include a butterfly garden, pond, windmill, marsh, play area, and trail.

Start indoors. The very helpful volunteers and staff are more than happy to help children hold some of the small animals. There are several friendly rabbits, turtles, snakes, lizards, and prairie dogs.

MAKE THE MOST OF YOUR TIME Various factors determine whether your little one gets to hold any given animal. An animal may be out for a party or a class or your child could be too young to hold it on his or her own. To prevent meltdowns, avoid promising snuggles with a specific bunny or turtle. But definitely do the indoor animal area before anything else, as most kids find it to be the star attraction.

228-06 Northern Blvd.,
Douglaston, Queens

 Free

 Sept–June, M–Sa 9–4:30, Su 9–3:30;
Closed Su in July, Aug, and some holidays

718/229–4000; www.alleypond.com

 2 and up;
art workshop 5 and up

In warmer months a walk around the quick trail is a must-do for all ages. It takes less than 10 minutes to stroll the flat, scenic boardwalk around the pond and marsh.

Take advantage of the weekend drop-in programs—one of the nicest features for visiting families. For younger kids, mostly 3–4, or 5–7, these short programs teach kids simple concepts like the frog's life cycle or how to care for caterpillars. For ages 8–12, recent programs have included Animal Care Trainee (the ABCs of animal care), Mad Scientist (answering important environmental questions), Young Chefs (cooking with a natural ingredient like honey), and APEC Safari.

If you like this sight, you may also like the Queens Zoo (#15).

EATS FOR KIDS

Naturally, the grounds here make an ideal picnic spot. Pick up some of the sandwiches locals rave about at **Malba Deli** (14524 14th Ave., tel. 718/746–9789) before heading over. For a sit-down meal, **Villagio Restaurante** (15007 14th Rd., tel. 718/747–1111) on Cross Island Parkway serves super-pleasing brick-oven pizzas and pastas at good prices.

KEEP IN MIND Taking the E or F train (Union Turnpike station) then the Q46 bus (Winchester Boulevard stop) will get you here, but a car is easier and faster. A short drive (less than three minutes) from the environmental center is the 657-acre Alley Pond Park. Not only will you find a deeply wooded, tranquil place with trails and NYC's tallest tree, you can also enjoy the Tri-State's largest ropes course, available by appointment only.

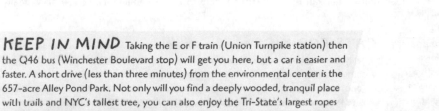

AMERICAN MUSEUM OF NATURAL HISTORY

67

To most, this is a ginormous world-class museum and planetarium. To New Yorkers, especially Upper West Side families, it's the world's coolest indoor playground.

In inclement weather, join them in the "Whale Room" and Discovery Center, both filled with kids getting wiggles out. On hot days screams of joy erupt as overheated kids run around the splash fountain on the water terrace.

If it's your family's first visit, you'll need to hit the highlights: Make a beeline for Fossil Hall, the world's largest collection of vertebrate fossils (85% of the museum's 1 million are actual fossils and not casts). On the way, ask your kids, "Are Dinosaurs extinct?" Answer: No. Birds are the modern wing of the dinosaur family. Watch the evolution film, then follow the dinosaur tracks to visit the towering T-Rex, Brontops, and others.

Another dramatic must-do? The Akeley Hall of African Mammals. Unless you've been 3 feet from an Alaskan Brown Bear or a herd of African elephants, you've never really

MAKE THE MOST OF YOUR TIME

This is one of the few NYC museums where the kids will be going strong far after you're ready for a rest. Plan to tag team with a spouse or caregiver, so one of you can go explore neighboring Central Park or rest on a park bench until its time to switch.

EATS FOR KIDS The Museum Food Court serves a wider variety and better quality of food than your typical museum cafeteria, including the kid-standard mac & cheese, chicken fingers, and pizza. Café on 1 also offers quick gourmet sandwiches, tasty salads, and drinks. For something more original, venture into the neighborhood (7 blocks away) to **Popover Café** (551 Amsterdam Ave., tel 212/595–8555). This spot is a tribute to the versatile popover, with all types of foods (salads, sandwiches, omelets) tucked inside. Or opt for a basket of plain popovers with the strawberry butter, a kid-pleasing combo.

Central Park West at 79th St.

 212/769-5100, 212/769-5200 museum programs and tickets, 212/769-5993 natural science center; www.amnh.org

 Suggested donation $15 ages 13 and up, $8.50 children 2–12; museum and space show $22 ages 13 and up, $13 children; IMAX extra

Daily 10–5:45, space shows daily 10:30–4:30, 1st F of mth 10:30–7

 2 and up

seen these magnificent animals up close. Thanks to the realistic dioramas, kids can safely study these creatures down to their whiskers.

Swing by the Rose Center to touch an actual meteor or see a Mars rover, then catch a show in the Hayden Planetarium. Right next door, the Hall of Gems satisfies any child with a love of sparkly things. Show them diamonds, opals, and the world's larges sapphire. The "Whale Room" (aka Hall of Biodiversity) still astounds even the most jaded visitor with its life-size blue whale hovering over other ocean life dioramas.

Finally, a favorite for kids under 11 is the Discovery Room, with tactile experiences to engage younger scientists. Do a scavenger hunt to find all the living things in the indoor tree, open doors and drawers to touch shells, insects, and more. The upstairs, for those over 8, offers microscopes to get a close look at nature.

If you like this sight, you may also like the National Museum of the American Indian (#31).

KEEP IN MIND If you can pull your kids away from the tempting gift shop, visit **Maxilla & Mandible** (451 Columbus Ave., tel. 212/724–6173). An emporium of natural items unlike any other, this shop holds piles of shells, fossils, bones, and bugs—almost all of which are real (well, except the human bones). Kids can find something they'll treasure for as little as $1.

THE ART FARM IN THE CITY

Living inside a slim brownstone on a relatively quiet part of the Upper East Side is a place you could consider Manhattan's only farm, with a little poetic license.

And to the kids that come here, this basement room, painted with apple trees and filled with all kinds of animals to hold and love, could just as well be a corner of Iowa.

You'll mostly find small mammals and reptiles in this indoor petting zoo, including hamsters, chinchillas, rabbits, mice, hermit crabs, geckos, or turtles. There are three ways to visit the animals. First, you can try a Drop In Playtime package. For 3 hours in the afternoon Monday–Thursday, the facility opens up to visitors who can do "animal time" for a few minutes or the whole drop-in time. Another option is on weekends: the Mornings on The Farm program (8 AM–10 AM) lets kids begin their day here. Using hay and other treats, kids feed and cuddle the animals.

MAKE THE MOST OF YOUR TIME Prices here are NOT pro-rated. To get the most for your animal drop-in time arrive as close to opening as possible. When money is no object, or you are going to be in NYC for more than a month or two, the adoption program saves time. Instead of rushing to be there at 8 AM on a weekend morning you can come in leisurely almost any time of day.

 419 E. 91st St.

 Prices vary by activity

 M–F 5:30 AM–10 PM, Sa–Su 8–8

212/410–3117;
www.theartfarms.org

1 and up

Finally, for longer term visitors, or people with fewer budget restrictions, the Part-Time Pet gives visiting-time flexibility. Designed to help city parents who want their children to have a pet but don't want the responsibility, kids are granted visiting rights to their chosen animal. Priced by the type of pet (ranges from a low of $130 for a hermit crab to $330 for a chinchilla), the program allows kids to visit their animal virtually anytime The Art Farm is open with a few weekend hours blocked. If your kids become attached to regular fluffytime, this is worth considering.

Although they do have other family-friendly activities, including art, music, and cooking programs, nothing compares to the chance to cuddle small creatures without leaving Manhattan.

If you like this sight, you may also like the Alley Pond Environmental Center (#68).

KEEP IN MIND
Being near the East River means being four long avenue blocks from any subway (at least until the 2nd Avenue line is completed). In winter, or with tired kids, spring for a cab and bring your smaller stroller.

EATS FOR KIDS The official NYC breakfast (and lunch, some might argue) is the bagel. So swing by **The Bagel Mill** (1700 1st Ave., tel. 212/426–0868) to sample the local goods for a cheap but decent breakfast. Stop and pick something up here if you are going to picnic in Carl Schurz Park overlooking the East River (eat-in is available as well). **Eli's Vinegar Factory** (431 E. 91st St., tel. 212/987–0885) is an informal café serving breakfast, pizza, sandwiches, soups, pastries, and coffee; upstairs there's a weekend brunch.

BOOKS OF WONDER AND CUPCAKE CAFE

Lured in by the powerful one-two punch of children's book and sweets, kids get so absorbed they barely make a peep—until they want money for cupcakes, that is.

This duo of indie kids' bookstore and upscale bakery puts all other chain equivalents to shame. Witness the book selection: Staff Picks reflect books chosen for quality and not just sell-ability. Next to childhood favorites, award winners, and currently popular titles, are the equally represented lesser-known gems. Expect a wide selection even among subjects getting no play in big chains (e.g., poetry, religion, African-American interest, and tricky topics like divorce). And, they have one of the most impressive collections of New York City–themed children's books to be found anywhere.

The kid-friendly atmosphere scores serious points. This place is very chill. Think library minus the tense silence. Sit in the wide aisles. Revel in the low ambient noise (and no piped music). Talk to each other. Read to each other. Laugh aloud. Even let toddlers

MAKE THE MOST OF YOUR TIME

This is the ideal place to tuck into when you want to kill some time. Got 20 minutes before a movie? An hour before dinner? Kids will get lost in the literature and you can finally get a minute to glance at your cell phone.

EATS FOR KIDS There are other restaurants in the area, but your kids will be rooted to the spot when they notice the three gigantic dancing cupcakes that represent **The Cupcake Cafe**'s colorful buttercream creations. And part of the appeal of coming here is eating one of their rich treats. You can practically smell the rich yellow and chocolate cake the minute you walk in the door. And best of all, the staff welcomes you to sit at a table eating your goodies while reading their books.

18 W. 18th St. and Broadway

 Free

M–Sa 10–7, Su 11–6

 212/989-3270;
www.booksofwonder.com

All ages

be toddlers—screaming and all. The staff spring into action, helping you find just the right books, but they're just as content to leave you in peace.

The events transform this from bookstore to community center. Sure, there are plenty of author signings from Pulitzer and Caldecott award winners. But you'll also find kids' concerts and creative workshops. Most holidays and special occasions have themed events.

If you like this sight, you may also like the New York Public Library (#22).

KEEP IN MIND It's hard for a full-priced bookstore to compete against discount vendors like Amazon, but Books of Wonder works hard to retain its customers with free gift wrapping and saving certificates with each purchase, sometimes $2 or $3 off your next purchase. Plus, you get the philanthropic glow of supporting an old-fashioned neighborhood shop that makes NYC the place it is.

BROADWAY ON A BUDGET

Reality check: Nobody living in New York City pays full price for Broadway tickets. And once you know about the plethora of discount ticket options, you won't either.

You may already be familiar with TKTS ticket booths as a way to get 20%–50% off face-value tickets. Don't expect to see the newest hit show offered, but virtually anything running for a year or more will be available at some point. The most popular (read: longest lines) Times Square Booth sits below a beautiful set of glass bleachers, giving a pep-rally view of Times Square. It sells day-of-performance tickets only. The South Street Seaport and Downtown Brooklyn booths sell tickets to evening performances on the day of the performance, and matinee the day before. The latter also sells tickets to Brooklyn performing arts events. Follow their Twitter feed (http://twitter.com/TKTS) to get show availability before trudging out to their locations. There is a non-musicals line that is much shorter if you are seeing a play.

What you may not know is that the Theater Development Fund (the organization behind TKTS) runs a membership discount ticket service ($30 annually) providing advance tickets

MAKE THE MOST OF YOUR TIME If you've ever hunted for online shopping coupons and discount codes, you'll be happy to know they exist for Broadway, too. Do an Internet search for "Discount Broadway Tickets" with the show's name, or search Web sites like www.broadwaybox.com before using any other method to get tickets. Broadway shows rarely go for less than $55; so if you can snag anything less than that online, you will save yourself some dough and several minutes standing in line or at the box office.

TKTS Times Square, Broadway and 47th St.;
South Street Seaport, 199 Water St.;
Downtown Brooklyn, 1 MetroTech Center,
corner Jay St. and Myrtle Ave.

 Usually 50%–75%
off regular price
plus $4 surcharge
per ticket

 Duffy Sq. M–Sa 3–8, plus W and Sa 10–
2, Su 11–7; Seaport M–Sa 11–6, Su 11–
4, Brooklyn T–Sa 11–6 (Closed 3 –3:30).

8 and up, but varies by show

212/912–9770; www.tdf.org

to many shows for $11–$39 a ticket for Broadway (and $9 for Off-Off-Broadway). Because it's open to students, teachers, union members, military, performing arts professionals, and more, chances are you or someone in your family qualifies.

The next best option is specialty or chance tickets. Many theaters offer Student Rush, Standing Room Only, and Lottery tickets. Check with individual theaters for policies and details. Seats can range from prime orchestra to partial view. Students with ID can often get relatively cheap tickets to even hit shows that are otherwise not discounted by going to the box office at a specified time (check with the individual theaters for details). Lottery tickets are available to winners picked in a drawing (each winner is entitled to 2 tickets). Anyone can get the limited availability SRO seats, which are usually designated standing areas behind the orchestra seats—they are typically available when the box office opens.

If you like Broadway, you may also like Symphony Space (#6).

KEEP IN MIND

Another inexpensive way to see well-known, long-running shows is to look for bookmark-shaped discount coupons, formerly called "twofers." They're distributed by store cash registers, near the TKTS lines, and sometimes in NYC elementary and preschool schools. Look for them at a local NYPL branch if all else fails. These coupons enable you to buy tickets for 20%–30% off shows for selected days and times.

EATS FOR KIDS Ninth Avenue has several good choices for families. In warm weather, eat at **Terazza Toscana**'s (742 9th Ave., tel. 212/315–9191) roof garden with an entire section for kids to hang out in while parents sip some vino. For a quick bite, walk over to the World Financial Center (49th/50th St. at 8th/9th Aves.) with its outdoor tables and benches and get Kobe hamburgers and crisp fries at **Mother Burger** (329 W. 49th St., tel. 212/757–8600).

BRONX ZOO

63

Unless you live near a mega-zoo, your kids deserve a visit here. The East Coast's answer to the San Diego Zoo, this is the largest urban wildlife park in the U.S. (4,000+ animals) and one that takes a humane, cage-free approach.

Come early, allow plenty of time, and bring comfortable walking shoes, you could easily spend a full three days here and still not do it all.

Visit the most popular attractions in the morning when the crowds are thinnest. These include the African Savannah with its giraffes, zebras, lions, and the three cubs born early 2010 (only available March 31–November 3); Congo Gorilla Forest, with its 20 lowland gorillas so remarkably human-like they often interact with visitors; and the Wild Asia Monorail, with elephants, rhinoceros, tigers, and other Asian animals in the 40 wooded acres.

KEEP IN MIND

Everyone loves baby animals. Be sure to check the Web site to find out the latest zoo newcomers your kids can coo over.

MAKE THE MOST OF YOUR TIME

The subway from Brooklyn and Manhattan takes at least 60 minutes to get here. But taking an express bus usually takes no more than 30 minutes. The BxM11 express bus stops along Madison Avenue, between 26th and 99th Streets, then travels directly to the Zoo's Bronx River entrance (Gate B). For your return trip, pick up the bus just outside the same gate at the MTA BxM11 sign (just before the underpass).

Bronx River Pkwy. and Fordham Rd., Bronx

 718/367–1010; www.wcs.org, www.bronxzoo.com

 $14 ages 13 and up, $10 children 3–12, children 2 and under free; rates change seasonally and annually; some attractions and special exhibits extra

Apr–Oct, M–F 10–5, Sa–Su and holidays 10–5:30; Nov–Mar, daily 10–4:30; Children's Zoo Apr–Oct

1 and up, Children's Zoo 8 and under

Then plan your route around some of the kids' favorites, including the bug carousel (insects substitute for horses), the World of Reptiles, the Children's Zoo, Jungle World, the Sea Lions, and the Bear habitat.

To save little feet, take the shuttle between Wild Asia and Zoo Center.

Family programs and activities are numerous, including Sea Lion Feedings, Primate Training, and Tiger Enrichment. But the biggest attraction is the Family Overnight Safari: After meeting some nocturnal creatures and doing zoo activities, kids sleep in tents and wake up to the sound of peacocks. These sell out months in advance, so book the minute they become available.

If you like this sight, you may also like the Central Park Zoo (#56).

EATS FOR KIDS The food at the zoo has only gotten worse in recent years. Although there are several on-site cafés for french fries and heat-lamp burgers, we suggest bringing snacks and spreading out on the picnic tables, then venturing from the zoo when dinner rolls around. If you're up for adventure, Arthur Avenue, aka The Bronx's Little Italy, is walking distance from the zoo. You can't go wrong at any of the restaurants lining this street, although local favorites seem to include **Dominick's** (2335 Arthur Ave., tel. 718/733–2807) and **Roberto's** (603 Crescent Ave., tel. 718/733–9503).

BROOKLYN BOTANIC GARDEN

Although a botanical garden might be enjoyable for adults, kids need a little help to see it as more than just a collection of green things, so it pays to do your homework and download the "Garden Exploration Activity Guide for Teachers" PDF guide under the "School Visits" section.

This guide helps families find avenues of approach to make the flora relevant to a kid's life. It is part conversation guide, part map, and it helps kids see how diverse and magnificent the plant world can be. It's also a great cheat sheet for organizing a family visit. The gardens can be done in any order, but the following are the can't-miss attractions.

The Children's Garden: The people who created this garden are all between 3 and 17, and your kids can join in the fun planting crops and flowers under the guidance of instructors. There is also craft-making and imaginative play.

The Discovery Garden: Kids are invited to have interactive experiences with natural objects, such as touching and smelling plants, digging for worms, or journeying through various habitats (woodlands, meadow, farm, wetland).

MAKE THE MOST OF YOUR TIME Taking the Harlem Line of Metro North (the trains leaving from Grand Central) will save at least 50 minutes round trip over the subway. Go on a weekend "City Ticket" and its only $3.50 per adult (kids are $0.75 each way on a Family Fare rate).

1000 Washington Ave., Brooklyn

 $8 adults, students 12 and up $4, under 12 free

 Mid-Mar–Oct, T–F 8–6, Sa–Su 10–6; Nov–mid-Mar, T–F 8–4:30, Sa–Su 10–4:30

718/623-7200, 718/623-7220 Discovery Programs; www.bbg.org

 All ages

Celebrity Path: Paved with stones inscribed with the names of famous Brooklynites, this path shows Brooklyn's past and present with names like Walt Whitman or Barbara Streisand. (Feel free to hum a few bars of "The Way We Were.")

Fragrance Garden: Have children close their eyes and smell their way around this garden, intentionally filled with plants that are recognizable by nose. Sniff your way around patchouli, lavender, peppermint, sage, basil, and more.

On Tuesdays and Thursdays there are drop-in, free activities in the Discovery Garden. Summer visitors should check out the cool moonlit walk to explore bats and other nocturnal wildlife (6+).

If you like this sight, you may also like the New York Botanical Garden (#27).

KEEP IN MIND
Not only are children under 12 free here, but senior citizens are free on Friday year-round, so bring the grandparents. Saturday is also free 10–12 except on days when special public programs are scheduled. Mid-November through February it's also a free-for-all, so if it's a mild day, consider checking out the garden as it prepares for winter.

EATS FOR KIDS Picnicking isn't allowed in the garden. Try the on-site **Terrace Café**, which serves lunch outdoors from spring to early fall and in the Steinhardt Conservatory late fall and winter. For deli sandwiches and its famous cheesecake, take a short ride to **Junior's Restaurant** (386 Flatbush Ave., tel. 718/852-5257), a classic '50s diner.

61

Walking across the Brooklyn Bridge is not only a way to span—and experience—two boroughs, it's also a way to span two worlds. Looking at the cable pattern, stone towers, wood planks, and original toll prices (5¢ for a cow or horse, 2¢ for a hog or sheep) transports you back to the New York of the 1800s.

And looking at the Manhattan skyline, with its steeples of commerce practically hitting the heavens, is a reminder of its central role in today's society.

A classic NYC family experience is walking across the Brooklyn Bridge into Brooklyn, eating lunch at the Fulton Ferry Landing, then taking the Water Taxi back to South Street Seaport. Full of stunning vistas, this long walk definitely works up an appetite.

Once across the bridge, follow the path down the steps to Washington Street. Turn left on Front Street and again on Old Fulton Street, where you'll find a long line at

EATS FOR KIDS
Grimaldi's (19 Old Fulton St., tel. 718/858–4300) is an ideal pizza place, but if its too crowded or you don't want to wait, there are several other good Italian restaurants lining the block.

MAKE THE MOST OF YOUR TIME The ideal time to do this expedition is starting around 11 AM. This will give you plenty of time to complete the walk and tour around. Alternatively, if you don't want to do South Street Seaport, going around 5 PM in summer will set you up for a gorgeous sunset from the pier before you leave. The walk itself is about 20 minutes with middle schoolers in tow, double that for toddlers or kids who aren't accustomed to long strolls.

Grimaldi's Pizza (19 Old Fulton St., tel. 718/858–4300). Arguably one of the best pizza places in the city, the wait is usually 30 minutes. After your meal, wander the neighborhood looking at the bookstores and boutiques. Get a small chocolate at the amazing chocolatier **Jacques Torres** (66 Water St., tel. 718/875–9772), but save it for later. Because the highlight of your kids' visit will certainly be the homemade ice cream found in the pier-side former school house, the **Brooklyn Ice Cream Factory** (Old Fulton St., Brooklyn, tel. 718/246–3963). Take your scoops or sundae to the brand new Brooklyn Bridge Park, a lovely stretch of waterfront greenery, playgrounds, benches, and (in summer) water features and pool. Then, hop the Water Taxi to South Street Seaport to head back to Manhattan.

If you like this sight, you may also like the South Street Seaport Museum (#9).

KEEP IN MIND If you've run out of energy in Brooklyn, the F train will take you back to most places in Manhattan. Also, there are a few benches scattered along the bridge should you need to take a breather.

BROOKLYN CHILDREN'S MUSEUM

This museum's heartbeat, like the Dodgers or Nathan's Hot Dogs, will always be 100% Brooklyn. The recent overhaul has done even more to infuse it with this eclectic borough's spirit.

The museum's biggest strength is its exploration of the modern American melting pot in all its hyphenated glory (e.g., Chinese-American, African-American). Before you do anything here, check out the info board for the day's programs. Typically there will be at least 5–7 things going on every day. On holidays there are themed programs that push way beyond the typical coloring sheet. Recent programs and events include Wacky Tuesday (science for 5 and under), Roving Animals (touch live animals from the museum's collection), Get Your Rhythm Going (creating music with a hand drum toy), and Tales for Tots (storytelling).

After entering through a neon-lit tunnel, head to World Brooklyn, a 4,000-square-foot exhibit highlighting the many vibrant cultures that call this borough home. It includes a streetscape of interactive storefronts from Brooklyn's own ethnic neighborhoods. Create a colorful costume

EATS FOR KIDS Visit the new **Kids Café** in the museum, which also opens onto the rooftop terrace for outdoor dining in good weather. Or try **Kingston Pizza** (259 Kingston Ave., tel. 718/774–7665) for a cheesy slice. **Eastern Chinese** (127 Kingston Ave., tel. 718/735–3408), also nearby, serves up Szechuan, Hunan, and Cantonese family favorites.

145 Brooklyn Ave., Brooklyn

 $7.50 per person

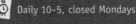 Daily 10-5, closed Mondays

 718/735-4400;
www.brooklynkids.org

 9 and under

for Caribbean Carnival, dish up a pretend pie at the pizzeria, or bake bread in the Mexican bakery.

Totally Tots, a spot for 5 and under, is a wonderland of sand and water play, climbing structures, art spaces, a reading nook, and a theater.

Neighborhood Nature, 7,000 square feet devoted to natural science, is all about getting in touch with nature, literally. Museum educators help visitors touch live horseshoe crabs and sea stars at the tide pool. In the community garden, get imaginary dirt under your nails as you plant, dig, and harvest play plants. Say hi to Fantasia (a 20-foot Python) before you make your way to the rest of the museum.

If you like this sight, you may also like the Children's Museum of Manhattan (#54).

MAKE THE MOST OF YOUR TIME

While a trip here is worth it at any time, take a moment online to look up the schedule so you won't walk in minutes late for a cool activity.

KEEP IN MIND If you are still jonesin' for kid-museum fun, try the **Jewish Children's Museum** (792 Eastern Parkway, tel. 718/467-0600). With its Game Show studio, pretend Kosher Supermarket and Kitchen, and hands-on exhibits celebrating Jewish holidays, biblical history, and the land of Israel, it's a museum like no other.

BROOKLYN MUSEUM

Notice that this museum's name is not followed by "of art." That's intentional, and it's good news for kids. Although it's grand in size (560,000 square feet), scope, and age (200-plus years), the focus is firmly on inclusion. Although some deride it as "populism," kids will enjoy a visit here far more than to most comparable (and if truth be told, stuffy) institutions of this magnitude.

The entrance—a new addition, resembling a glass UFO that landed at the base of the gigantic neoclassical stone building—is a hint of the museum's fresh/modern and welcoming attitude toward visitors of all ages.

Begin on the third floor with its way cool collection of Egyptian artifacts (aka mummies). After that, check out the current exhibit. Usually they're visually stimulating enough to appeal to kids. Recent exhibits have included Murakami, an anime-influenced artist who creates action-figure-like sculptures with bold colors and oversize features; a photographic

EATS FOR KIDS

The **Museum Café** is open almost as long as the museum. **Tom's Restaurant** (782 Washington Ave., tel. 718 636–9738) is a quick walk away. This neighborhood institution has loads of kid-friendly fare.

MAKE THE MOST OF YOUR TIME The museum is part of the
Heart of Brooklyn initiative linking some of the borough's best attractions. Literally next door are the Brooklyn Botanic Garden (#62), the main branch of the Brooklyn Public Library, and Prospect Park and its zoo (#s 19 and 18). A few blocks away is the Brooklyn Children's Museum. Kids will tolerate a max of 2–3 hours here, so plan on spending the rest of your day running around outdoors or doing the Children's Museum.

200 Eastern Pkwy., Brooklyn

718/638–5000;
www.brooklynart.org,
www.brooklynmuseum.org/education

Suggested donation $10 adults,
$6 students and seniors, children
under 12 free

W–F 10–5, Sa–Su 11–6, 1st Sa of mth
11–11; free after 5 PM except Sept

6 and up

collection of rock musicians; and a survey of the best of the Museum of Modern Art's Costume Collection: 80 dressed mannequins sporting chic dresses, pants, frilly shoes, and period hats.

If you still have their attention, go to the Elizabeth A. Sackler Center for Feminist Art. The specific political and socio-cultural messages will be lost on kids under 10. Instead, stick with a simple message that most museums don't have many pieces of art by women. Kick off a conversation about women artists: "Have we seen any pictures this trip made by women? Are there any famous female artists?" Then, point out how this is one of the few places where art by women has a home.

The Arts of Africa and Pacific Islands have objects that amuse kids with oversized limbs or heads and extreme facial expressions. Figures like the one from the Nicobar Islands or the monkey for Mbra are like other cultures' Polly Pockets.

If you like this sight, you may also like the Museum of Modern Art (#33).

KEEP IN MIND Don't make a day of it. Make a night of it! The Museum's premier event for all ages, First Saturdays, takes place 5–11 PM every month except September. This family-friendly event is free, and features music in the galleries, art-making projects, films, performances, and gallery talks, and ends with a dance party that feels like a giant block party. Flat-rate parking is a bargain after 5 PM, and the **Museum Café** stays open so you can enjoy dinner with the family.

THE CATHEDRAL CHURCH OF
ST. JOHN THE DIVINE

Regardless of your religious affiliation, you gotta love a place in the middle of Manhattan that's so big the Statue of Liberty could fit under the dome without her pedestal. (It's the world's largest cathedral at 121,000 square feet.)

A walk around the exterior will get imaginations spinning, thanks to some pretty funky architectural elements. In addition to the usual creepy gargoyles, species-confused animals, and saints and martyrs with no eyes, there are some figures that are simply baffling. The workman with hardhat and measuring tape; Hamlet holding poor Yorick's skull; a baby's head emerging from a flower? All things weird and wonderful.

A walk around inside reinforces the church's inclusive motto, "A House of Prayer for All People." Each of its chapels is dedicated to a different national, ethnic, or social group, including The American Poet's Corner (where 30 writers have been inducted including Walt Whitman, Emily Dickinson, and Robert Frost), the FDNY memorial (originally honoring

EATS FOR KIDS Before you venture toward healthier foods, get some cookies at **The Hungarian Pastry Shop** (1030 Amsterdam Ave., tel. 212/866–4230). A neighborhood institution for a zillion years, it's pretty much frozen in time, from the menu (painted on upper cabinets and never changed) to the specialities (baklava, streudels, cookies) to the cash-only policy. Or pop into **Whole Foods** (808 Columbus Ave., tel. 212/222–6160) to cobble together a healthy picnic for the Cathedral grounds.

firefighters killed in a 1966 fire but now expanded to be a tribute to 9/11 heros), and the St. Savior's chapel to honor Christian communities of the East, which includes two Buddhist temple cabinets to honor Asians as well.

On Saturdays do one of the nature- or medieval-based workshops. Recent ones have included Stained Glass, Medieval Arts (such as designing gargoyles), and Wonders of the Sun (making sundials).

On the vertical tour, kids 12 and up climb 124 feet via spiral staircase to the top for the magnificent view of Manhattan.

If you like this sight, you may also like the Rubin Museum (#12).

MAKE THE MOST OF YOUR TIME

Call to make workshop reservations in advance, as they can fill up quickly, especially in winter. Plan to spend 20–40 minutes outside exclusive of participating in any of the organized tours. The wonderful peace-themed children's sculpture garden is a favorite on a warm day.

KEEP IN MIND Check the calendar for seasonal events, the Blessing of the Animals (October) being by far the most popular. In the past zebras, elephants, and of course thousands of NYC pets have been blessed here. The Blessing of the Bikes in April is similar but far less fluffy. And the Procession of the Ghouls (NOT for young children or those easily scared) may be the most bizarre Halloween event to take place inside a church. Typically, this is followed by a screening of the silent film *Nosferatu* accompanied by a church organ.

CENTRAL PARK

57

In warm weather your kids could easily spend their whole vacation in Central Park and still not do everything this communal backyard has to offer.

The southernmost square mile contains attractions that could be stand-alone all-day activities: The Central Park Zoo, The Central Park Kid's Zoo, and Wollman Rink (in summer this becomes the Victorian Gardens amusement park) are the biggest ones. Families anchor their visit around one venue and explore from that spot.

Other top sights include the Marionette Theater (advance ticket reservations are required, 79th St. Transverse, tel. 212/988-9093), the Chess & Checkers House (lending out board games), and the Conservatory Water (renting model sailboats). Belvedere Castle (79th St. Transverse, tel. 212/772-0210) holds a weather station and the Henry Luce Nature Observatory. Dash through the adorable Dairy Visitor Center and Gift Shop (65th St., mid-park, tel. 212/794-6564) for park information and merchandise.

MAKE THE MOST OF YOUR TIME

Newcomers spend more time trying to figure out how to get between places than actually enjoying them. Prevent that and get the detailed official Central Park Conservancy map in advance or pick up one up at the Dairy, so you can spend more time at each site instead of finding it.

EATS FOR KIDS The **Boathouse** restaurant has lovely views of the lake and equally lovely food, but requires advance reservations and is definitely not for young kids. Luckily, you can get practically the same view but with a more chaotic kid-friendly atmosphere at **The Boathouse Café** (Central Park, tel. 212/517-2233). For the ideal picnic, head to the Sheep Meadow, where you'll find a **Pain Quotidian** (Central Park, tel. 646/233-3768) ready to sell you a premade picnic package or individual sandwiches, salads, treats, and beverages.

Bordered by 5th Ave., Central Park West, 59th St., and 110th St.

 212/360–3444; www.centralparknyc.org

 Free; some attractions charge

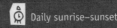 Daily sunrise–sunset

All ages

Of the twenty-plus playgrounds in and around Central Park, Hecksher is the most magnificent, with castle towers and a moat (when its over 80 degrees, sprinklers and "rivers" run through them); a giant sandbox with a climbing web, tunnels, and swings; two astroturf picnic areas; slides; swings; and four recently built clean bathrooms.

A small path away is the 1903 Friedsam Memorial Carousel (Center Dr. and 65th St., tel. 212/879–0244), with some of the world's largest hand-carved horses. To its left (west) are baseball fields where Broadway stars and stagehands play together in leagues every weekend.

As you meander, allow plenty of time for kids to climb sculptures (especially Balto the dog and Alice in Wonderland), watch the buskers, climb rocks, lounge in the Sheep Meadow, or just people-watch.

If you like this sight, you may also like Prospect Park (#19).

KEEP IN MIND This glorious park receives virtually no public funds (in other words, no tax dollars go toward its upkeep). Becoming a member of The Central Park Conservancy is not only a way to show your appreciation for this oasis, its a good way to get discounts. For your $35 membership you can get 10% off at several local restaurants (including Mickey Mantle's), 10% off room rates at many NYC hotels, and 2 for 1 admission to Victorian Gardens Monday–Thursday.

CENTRAL PARK ZOO

"Savage Brutes at Large!" So ran a headline in the 1874 *NY Herald* about animals escaping from the Central Park Zoo and injuring 48 people.

Turns out the article was a hoax. No matter. The idea of the zoo's residents running wild down urban streets remains a popular motif. Especially with children who delight in seeing movies like *Madagascar* (watch it before a visit here).

And the city's most popular small zoo (almost 7 acres) deserves the accolade. Although compact, it has several very popular animals and is easy to navigate in a few hours, barring congestion.

Monkeys, polar bears, penguins, tropical birds, and seals are some of the most popular residents. Here are some tips for making it through the five areas:

Unless you also want to feel caged, too, plan an early-afternoon weekday visit, when school groups have thinned and there aren't so many local families and visitors.

MAKE THE MOST OF YOUR TIME This combined with a visit to the Tisch Children's Zoo is easily a 3– to 5-hour adventure, even for restless kids. Since your admission price gets you into both places, you may want to break your visit into two. Start with the highlights at the main zoo, then let kids feed the animals and play on the climbing structures at the kids' zoo. Then head back to the main zoo when the crowds thin to do the more subtle attractions like the red panda.

For the best view of the sea lion feeding, get there at least 20 minutes early to snag a spot up against the railing on the north side of the tank, where the handlers dole out fish. Check the Web site for the most updated feeding times. Along the way to the polar bears, look at the new snow leopard exhibit, head down the steps to be inches away from a polar bear, and then chill out with local families who flock (no pun intended) to the penguin house on hot summer days.

The Rain Forest brings the tropics indoors. With jungle plants, waterfalls, and colorful birds, kids will happily spend 20 minutes in here or more.

Visit the Tisch Children's Zoo with kids 9 and under. A combo petting zoo and playspace, this spot contains a few kid-friendly farm animals (bring quarters to buy food!); photo ops like big bunny cutouts; and a well-designed climbing web where kids get their wiggles out while balancing on rope.

If you like this sight, you may also like the Prospect Park Zoo (#18).

KEEP IN MIND
Taking a pedicab around the park is not only a novel way for kids to get a tour of the rest of this magnificent space, it is a good way to get over to your next destination (F.A.O. Schwarz, anyone?) and avoid the misuse of horses.

EATS FOR KIDS The once outstanding café is now best avoided. Instead, for a breakfast/brunch/anytime treat, go to **Norma's** in the Parker Meriden (188 W. 57th St., tel. 212/708–7460). Watch your kids eyes bug out when dishes like the PB&C Waffle 'Wich (Chocolate Waffle with a Peanut Butter and Toffee Crunch Filling) or Crunchy French Toast (Covered with Warm Caramel Sauce) arrive at the table. To lessen the glucose bomb, you can pair these with one of their healthy if still eccentric options like the Magic Mushroom Grilled Cheese Sandwich.

CHELSEA PIERS

This place may be greeted with bafflement by kids from the 'burbs, and some parents as well. Why pay relatively high prices for indoor sports facilities when there are cheap and spacious options at home?

Because by offering classes in everything from gymnastics to ice skating, this place embraces a wide range of activities to suit every personality, much like NYC itself.

While the New York City government has done nothing short of a miraculous job upgrading the city's athletic facilities, demand still far outweighs supply, and things can get crowded. On a positive note, it is convenient to have facilities for most major sports in one location, and that's a real treat in winter, when playing outdoors is not feasible.

KEEP IN MIND
Make an appointment to get a manicure or pedicure at the Chelsea Piers Spa while your child is in a drop-in class for a little luxurious treat.

MAKE THE MOST OF YOUR TIME
Call in advance to find out when drop-in classes or events take place. The Web site is not updated as often as the schedule. Unfortunately, there is no opportunity to join activities already in progress and no informal facilities available for the general public.

On cold days, plan on taking a taxi in at least one direction. The nearest subway stop is a bit of a schlep, and buses are not frequent.

Chelsea Piers is 28 acres placed on top of, you guessed it, four piers jutting out over the Hudson. Although there's a spot for almost all sports, most of the space is tied up for ongoing classes or leagues.

The sports available on an ad-hoc basis include SkyRink for ice skating, a golf driving range, a bowling alley, an indoor playground for toddlers 6 months–4 years ("Little Athletes Exploration Center"), and batting cages. Adults only can get day passes to a health club, spa, and pool with remarkable views.

If you like this sight, you may also like Karma Kids Yoga (#41).

EATS FOR KIDS The High Line, a newly converted railtrack-to-park space, is a short walk and a good picnic spot, especially after picking up goodies (everything from artisanal cheeses to frilly cupcakes) at the 20+ vendors in **Chelsea Market** (75 9th Ave. between 15th and 16th Sts.). The market also has a few café tables if the weather doesn't support picnic plans. **The Park** (118 10th Ave., tel. 212/352–3313) has pizza, salads, pasta, and plenty of room for kids to roam. Adults have dishes like calamari salad, seared tuna Niçoise, and lentil salad on baby arugula.

CHILDREN'S MUSEUM OF MANHATTAN

54

When property values skyrocketed, NYC families (especially in Manhattan) lost affordable indoor playspaces.

The CMOM (as its known to locals) is a victory in playrooms for the people. Although it far prefers to see itself as a museum that educates and increases awareness of other cultures, most parents of kids 6 and under see it as a giant indoor playground. Most locals keep their fingers crossed that the ground floor exhibit will be something climbable and touchable.

In winter, the third floor (PlayWorks) is jammed with kids under 6 trying on firefighter gear, climbing the firetruck, jumping on the dragon, making movies, throwing balls off the tower, driving the bus, playing with sand or water, and just generally doing the glorious mayhem you don't want your furniture subjected to.

The second most-popular spot, Adventures with Dora and Diego, has features geared toward toddlers and slightly older kids. There's a car to sit in, a slide, a musical instrument area, a "bed," a telephone, and other accoutrements of Dora's world.

MAKE THE MOST OF YOUR TIME Unless your child needs constant supervision, you'll be spending most of your time sitting on the floor with other parents as kids play autonomously. Bring a book or other diversion, you'll be glad you did by the 2nd or 3rd hour of indoor play.

Tisch Building, 212 W. 83rd St.

 $10 ages 1 and up, $7 seniors, free 1st Friday of the mth 5–8

 T–Fr and Sun 10–5, Sa 10–7

 212/721–1234; www.cmom.org

Infant–8

The top floor is for public programs. Almost every hour there is an art class, circle time, storytime, or performance. Half are appropriate for 4 and younger (generally held in the morning) and the other for 5 and above (in the afternoon).

The ground floor has rotating exhibits. Although these are no doubt carefully conceived and executed for the enlightenment of children, most families judge them by playground standards. For example, a recent Clifford exhibit was a big hit because of the climb-on lighthouse and gigantic red dog. The more recent Ancient Greece exhibit was significantly less popular with its displays.

In summer City Splash invites young visitors to explore the physical properties of water as they splash, pour, float, and play.

If you like this sight, you may also like the Brooklyn Children's Museum (#60).

KEEP IN MIND So much to do, so little time? Leave the stroller at home or in the car, and avoid the long lines at the coat/stroller check.

EATS FOR KIDS Only 10 feet away, **Cafe LaLo** (201 W. 83rd St., tel. 212/496–6031) has good French café specialties like quiche, belgian waffles, eggs, and frittatas. Kids and adults especially love going for a real hot chocolate (no powder used here!) paired with croissants. Since food is not allowed inside the museum, the best picnic option is to grab something at the deservedly famous **Zabar's** (2245 Broadway, tel. 212/787–2000) and either head to the Tecumseh Playground (Amsterdam Ave./77th St.) or duck into the West Side Community Garden (123 W. 89th St.), a serene block-long spot of greenery, flowers, and benches.

CHILDREN'S MUSEUM OF THE ARTS

By the time you are reading this, the museum may have moved to a bigger space—and that's great news. The staff and programs are spectacular, but it's hard for the drop-in visitor to tell, as the space is so small and in need of renovation. Until the move, focus on the workshops and open art studio, and skip the ball room or other free play spaces.

All the instructors are "teaching artists," practicing artists who also have serious kid-people skills. They know what they're doing, and they're delighted to be able to share their skills with your little ones.

Make the most of your trip here by going right up to the Open Art Studio. Every Wednesday through Sunday (the museum's open hours) kids can use the materials available to make paintings, sculptures, and collages. In the daily guided workshops an artist works with your child in a more structured setting to create art often tied to a theme or subject. Recent projects have included Recycled Sun Catchers, Quilt Design, and "Underneath,"

MAKE THE MOST OF YOUR TIME

Be sure to find out what time programs that interest your child will be held and schedule your day accordingly.

EATS FOR KIDS Get healthy, organic food at affordable prices at **Spring Street Natural** (62 Spring St., tel. 212/966–0290). For kids who are slightly more adventurous, **The Smile** (26 Bond St., tel. 646/329–5836) has well-priced small plates and sandwiches edging on the novel for local picnics or to eat in.

 182 Lafayette St.

 $10 ages 1–65, Th 4–6
"Pay as You Wish"

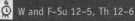 W and F–Su 12–5, Th 12–6

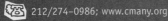 212/274-0986; www.cmany.org

 1–10

using art to explore the concept of what's underneath. The Performing Arts Gallery is notable as a place where kids can create their own theatrical performance.

If you're are lucky enough to be in the city on a summer weekend, get a sense of their real potential and catch the free ferry to Governor's Island (in lower Manhattan) to their Governor's Island Art Outpost. Not only do you get to experience one of the only urban islands in the world that is still devoid of commercial entities, condos, and corporations, but at the outpost kids participate in a themed art project with some of the city's best teaching artists. Themes change each month, and recent ones have included piñata making, wire sculptures, and robot costumes.

If you like this sight, you may also like the Children's Museum of Manhattan (#54).

KEEP IN MIND Got a momentous birthday coming up? Splurge on an art in the evening birthday party. For $650 plus gratuity, 15 children get the run of the museum, choice of an art project, and two birthday party artists.

CONEY ISLAND

52

"Step Right Up! See a fire-breathing woman swallow torches right before your eyes!" Yes, you'll actually hear carnival barkers here, and that's all a part of the nostalgic fun. Coney Island may no longer be able to outshine big-league amusement parks, but it's still an absolute kids' favorite.

Begin with Luna Park, a brand-new amusement park with 19 new rides. This is the only place in the world to ride Air Race, an airplane thrill that subjects bodies to 4 G's of force as it vertically spins them 360 degrees. Family rides are closer to the boardwalk.

Spend the hottest part of the day at the beach, or visit the Aquarium to escape the midday sun. In the afternoon, stroll the Boardwalk and play in the playground on the way to a Brooklyn Cyclones baseball game. This talented minor-league team is just part of the attraction; kids can also experience face painting, cheerleaders, magicians, raffles, T-shirt giveaways, ball tosses, fireworks, and running the bases.

EATS FOR KIDS Make the 60-minute subway ride go faster by bringing a nutritious snack to eat on the train. It'll help balance the avalanche of sweets to come. When you get there, the boardwalk is bursting with crinkle fries, cotton candy, funnel cakes, Italian ices, or candy apples, which are all part of the experience. You'll be hard-pressed to find a true sit-down dining experience without venturing off the main drag to Brighton Beach, unless you want pizza at **Totonno's** (1524 Neptune Ave., between W. 15th and W. 16th, tel. 718/372–8606).

Southern tip of Brooklyn

 Brooklyn Tourism and Visitors Center (718/802–3846; www.visitbrooklyn.org); Coney Island USA (718/372–5159; www.coneyisland.com)

 Free; amusement park rides vary

 Attraction hrs vary by season

1 and up

Lively traditional circus sideshows, complete with a fire-eater, sword swallower, snake charmer, and contortionist, are featured at Sideshows by the Seashore (W. 12th St. and Surf Ave., tel. 718/372–5159), the last standing ten-in-one sideshow in the country. Upstairs from the sideshows, you can find the Coney Island Museum (open Friday–Sunday 12 to 5), which contains exhibits spotlighting historic Coney Island and related memorabilia. An extensive array of tourist information and literature is also available here. Before you leave, make your Coney Island day complete by eating at Nathan's and getting a candy apple or taffy from William's Candy Shop—neither of which look much different than they did on opening day.

If you like this sight, you may also like Victorian Gardens (#3).

MAKE THE MOST OF YOUR TIME
Like a carnival, Coney Island is a place to visit in season. In summer the rides are open, the beach has lifeguards. Leave the watch at home and expect to spend at least 6 hours having a ball here.

KEEP IN MIND Luna Park may be the newest amusement area, but Deno's has the highest and one of the oldest rides. The Wonder Wheel gives great views of the ocean, the Manhattan Skyline, and Coney Island. It has only stopped once in its 90-year history (on July 13, 1977, during the Great NYC Blackout). Younger kids should stick to the stationary cars. And, of course, the Cyclone, a nostalgic wood rollercoaster, can still give a plunging thrill that competes with modern hydraulic giants.

EL MUSEO DEL BARRIO

At El Museum del Barrio's grand re-opening in 2009 the CEO described how the building's masonry was replaced by glass so the city's light could shine in while the energy of El Museo shines out, and you may feel a little boost when you gaze at it.

Rafael Montañez Ortiz founded the museum in 1969. The goal of the organization was to reflect the Latino cultural experience, which at the time wasn't represented in NYC's mainstream museums. And it does a wonderful job of connecting a disparate community through Puerto Rican, Caribbean, and Latin American art. If that sounds serious, don't worry. Even kids too young to understand this political and cultural context will naturally be drawn to the bright colors and tangible folk art.

The permanent collection contains 6,500 objects representing over 800 years of Latino history and culture through prints, drawings, paintings, sculpture, photographs, film, video, works on paper, and artifacts. Young visitors will enjoy the dolls, animal sculptures, and fur baseball glove, and other whimsical items. Older kids may particularly like the

EATS FOR KIDS

Stay at the museum and eat at **El Cafe** to get regional specialties like chilled tomato soup with cilantro or arepa con carne. To fully immerse them in the Latino experience, try tapas and Puerto Rican specialties at **Camaradasel Barrio Bar and Restaurant** (2241 1st Ave. at 115th, tel. 212/348–2703).

MAKE THE MOST OF YOUR TIME A visit here should take about two hours, leaving plenty of time to catch a Children's Read Aloud program at the Aguilar Branch of the New York Public Library (174 E. 110th St., tel. 212/534–2930) or other kids' events frequently scheduled here. Also close by is the Guggenheim Museum (1071 5th Ave., tel. 212/423–2500).

works on paper, or the paintings and sculptures. A favorite piece of eye-catching color and energy is *La Cama,* a sculpture of an ornate bed by Pepon Osorio. Signage throughout the museum is in Spanish and English.

Three popular family days are held throughout the year, with children's activities for visitors tall and small. The Three Kings Day Parade in January is a sight to see. Students and organizations may register to march in the event, or just come on down and watch the pageantry and parade. In June the museum is a major stop in Manhattan's Museum Mile event, with free admission to view the current exhibitions, as well as live music and dancing. November's Family Day includes live music, art making, dance, gallery tours, and other children-friendly activities. During summer there is a popular Summer Nights free concert series.

If you like this sight, you may also like the Rubin Museum (#12).

KEEP IN MIND For a quiet stroll or calming break in your touring, visit Central Park's nearby Conservatory Garden (enter at 5th Ave. and 105th St.). Few know of the walkway under the pergola of this 6-acre formal garden, decorated with medallions commemorating the original 13 states. Find the pergola by looking for the geyser fountain in front.

ELLIS ISLAND

Think back to the last three minutes of your life. Now imagine that in that same amount of time it would be decided whether you lived or died. Whether you ever saw your family again. Whether you went back to a life of poverty or had a chance at fortune.

That is exactly what happened to immigrants who landed on Ellis Island. In the time it took to walk up the main staircase and speak to an immigration officer, a decision was made whether an immigrant could start a promising new life or would have to return to their old, almost certainly difficult one.

And for many families, chances are high that an ancestor came through Ellis Island—making the immigration experience a personal one for you and your children. The National Park Service has done an outstanding job making this a compelling place for kids by simply allowing its inherent drama to unfold.

MAKE THE MOST OF YOUR TIME The audio tour is de riguer to make the proverbial walls talk. That means you should set aside at least three hours, including the round-trip ferry ride. Families with kids over 12 might want to consider combining this with a visit to the Statue of Liberty, but those with younger kids should stick with one site at a time. Unlike those for the Statue of Liberty, tickets for same-day Ellis Island ferry rides are easy to get (the monument is free, you only pay for the ride and the audio tour).

New York Harbor, Ferry leaves from South Ferry in Battery Park

 Free; ferry fees $12 ages 13 and up; $5 children 4–12; $10 seniors

Daily 8–2, ferry daily every hour; open daily except December 25

 Tickets and monument passes 877-LADY TIX; www.statuecruises.com; Ellis Island information 212/363-3200; www.nps.gov

7 and up

Doing the audio tour is a must with children. It will take you through all the rooms, and along the way they'll absorb Ellis Island's significance through the minutiae—the diversity of foods cooks needed to make, the baggage people brought, the toys and games children played with. During the tour they'll hear actual Ellis Island immigrants tell their own stories.

Two personal activities not to miss: First, search the passenger manifest and port records to see if you can find family members (this can be done for free online as well). Second, go to the metal wall outside the back door with a paper and pencil. If you can find an ancestor's name, have kids do a rubbing as a souvenir. Once on Ellis Island, you can stay as long as you like—until closing time.

If you like this sight, you may also like the Statue of Liberty (#7).

KEEP IN MIND For an absolutely one-of-a-kind souvenir, honor one of your family's immigrant ancestors by putting their name ($150) on the Wall of Honor.

EATS FOR KIDS The Ellis Island Cafe is a stellar example of what every attraction should have. There is a good selection of burgers, salads, sandwiches, and fish. They strive to include as many organic and healthy options as possible. Most are made fresh daily. On warm days, sit at the terrace tables for a great view of Lower Manhattan.

EMPIRE STATE BUILDING

From *Sleepless in Seattle* to *Gossip Girl,* movies and TV shows have built up the romance of this iconic building where characters race to the top for a fateful rendezvous. What none of those scenes show is the Byzantine process to get to that observation deck—something far more arduous with a hot, tired, or hungry child in tow.

Yes, you come to see one of the world's most amazing urban views, but you'll spend ten times longer getting there than seeing it. In other words, the *only* way to do this building with younger children is by bringing distractions and refreshments.

Rent the audio tour for everyone over 6. Disregard the narrator's instruction to start it on the elevator. Begin listening immediately. As you make your way up, you'll learn the exciting history of the building's construction (the 1,454-foot-tall structure was built in a year and 45 days for $41 million) and the heated competition between it and the Chrysler Building to earn the coveted title of world's tallest building. The tour goes beyond

KEEP IN MIND Top of the Rock, the top of Rockefeller Center just 10 blocks north, has an excellent view without the wait. In fact, some people prefer the view here, as it includes the Empire State Building in your sightline. Timed entry tickets can be purchased online and on-site.

MAKE THE MOST OF YOUR TIME There are five different lines to get to the 86th floor. The first is outdoors and can range from seconds to half an hour. The second, third, and fourth are all to buy tickets and get to the first elevator. On the final line, winding around ropes on the 80th floor, is unfortunately the slowest. Buying an express pass ($45) is a worthwhile investment. It allows you to bypass all these lines (except security) and get right to the top. Otherwise, go early in the morning (around 8 AM) or early evening for fewer crowds.

350 5th Ave., at 34th St.

 212/736-3100; www.esbnyc.com

 $20 adults, $14 children 6–11, under 5 free, $18 seniors; $45 express ticket for all ages

 Daily 8 AM–2 AM, last elevator at 1:15 AM

 3 and up

facts and figures, giving a sociological spin to the icon. First-time New York visitors may want to buy the panoramic graphic ($5) showing all the major buildings you'll see from the top.

The view from the 86th-floor observatory is full-on magnificent. It's a viewpoint you'll rarely see outside of nature itself. On a sunny day you can see 80 miles in all directions. The audio tour will point out most of the major landmarks familiar to kids from movies or TV (e.g., Brooklyn Bridge) and then some. (Unless money is no object, take a pass on the Skyride and the 102nd-floor observatory.)

If you like this sight, you may also like Rockefeller Center and the Ice Rink (#13).

EATS FOR KIDS The **Breslin Bar and Restaurant** (16 W. 29th St., tel. 646/214–5788) is a dark, wood-paneled pub with a noir vibe. Expect a laundry list of pig products: ham, beans baked in lard, other unmentionables. However, it also has an outstanding selection of healthier local or artisanal foods that are both impeccably prepared and well sourced, including market salads, goat-cheese tarts, and buffalo mozzarella. What will particularly delight the kids are the snacks you can get with lunch: malt vinegar and sea salt crisps, caramel popcorn, or boiled peanuts cooked in pork fat.

F.A.O. SCHWARZ

 This toy store still has the eye candy to knock out kids—although it's hovered a bit closer to over-the-medium than over-the-top since its bankruptcy and subsequent purchase by Toys"R"Us. Still, new visitors won't know any of the glam is gone, and there are enough specialized and oversized toys to impress even the most jaded kids. Be sure to watch the film *Big* before taking your kids here to up the wow factor.

Begin by getting the obligatory photo with the iconic toy soldier doorman. Then dive into the huge oversize-stuffed-animal section, surely rivaling Noah's Ark. Life-size giraffes, 8-foot grizzlies, 5-foot zebras, lions, and polar bears all populate this area. Next, ride up to the second floor to jump on the iconic big keyboard. During crowded holiday periods there's a line, but typically it's less than a five-minute wait to tickle the "ivories" with your toes.

From here you can break off into thematic toylands or customize your new playthings at Build-a-Bear-esque workshops. At Styled by Me Barbie, design a Barbie and have her plastic-

MAKE THE MOST OF YOUR TIME To avoid crowds, shop weekdays before lunch, or during the early afternoon and on weekends, the earlier the better. Also, if there's a wait to enter the 5th Avenue doors, skip the line by going to Madison and 58th. The doors there are virtually line-free.

mold-injected goodness in your hot hands in less than five minutes. The Muppet Whatnot Workshop enables kids to create their own "whatnot" (basically TV extras) by picking from a much wider selection of facial and body features than Barbie boasts. Pink Boa Hair, Furry Orange Tunic, Monster Big Green Nose with Fangs, and Yellow Eyes with Bushy Eyebrows are just a few of the options.

Trying to compete with the new candy boutique trend, they've opened F.A.O. Schweetz, with wondrous piles of toy-themed candy, including mints shaped like Mario Brothers and gigantic collector's edition Pez dispensers. For a cheap souvenir, buy an F.A.O.-brand container and fill it with candy, then refill it at home with your favorites.

If you like this sight, you may also like Toys"R"Us (#5).

KEEP IN MIND
Buy the big piano (or at least the $79 replica toy of it) to take home and you'll have a New York City souvenir that's truly iconic.

EATS FOR KIDS To get a real NYC experience, squeeze into the teeny **Viand Coffee Shop** (2130 Broadway, tel. 212/877-2888). It has the usual diner suspects—grilled cheese, gyros, meat loaf platters—but it's so teeny you'll wonder how people eat (and live) like this. For an equally good variety but a more spacious dining room, head west to **Mangia** (50 W. 57th St., tel. 212/582-5882) and indulge in antipasto, quesadillas, smoothies, or salads. In warm weather, grab a street table to do some serious people-watching.

FORBIDDEN PLANET

Visiting this manga mecca is a must for superhero-crazed kids and adults who fondly remember the glory days of Spider-Man pajamas.

Comic books are just the starting point at this emporium, with a virtually unparalleled variety of action figures and accessories, anime/manga collectables, apparel, DVDs, games, gundam (robots), magazines, plush toys, posters, statues, and toys. Fanboys are impressed by the way it bridges the gap between indies, underground, and mainstream comics, carrying some that no one else does. Others stare at the glass-encased rarities similar to a *Superman* #1. Adults and teens can easily spend an hour browsing the first-floor shelves (new comics come out on Wednesdays and can draw a big crowd). Unless you want your kids asking, "Mommy, what does A-Team Shotgun Wedding mean?", ask staff to help point you toward the much smaller range of age-appropriate graphic novels scattered about and completely avoid the horror and very graphic sexuality (e.g., "American Virgin") sections.

KEEP IN MIND
A 10% discount is offered to students (with IDs) and people who mention Yelp.

MAKE THE MOST OF YOUR TIME
If kids are old enough to be left alone here, walk one block south to **The Strand** (826 Broadway, tel. 212/473–1452). Claiming to have 18 miles of new, used, rare, and out-of-print books, this is by far New York City's biggest indie bookstore. With prices starting at $1 and most books at least 50% off list, and a selection that gets well beyond the mainstream, its a bibliophile's dream. At least for those people who haven't bought iPads and Kindles yet.

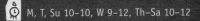

The areas kids will really love include the action figures (everything ranging from an $18 Captain Marvel action figure to a $180 GI Joe Cobra Throne, to the ultra-collectable $300 Indiana Jones vs Mola Ram); toys (Lego kits, tin toys, and plush dolls); games (board, card, and role playing); and apparel (an $18 tee turns your kid into Captain America).

If you like this sight, you may also like Books of Wonder and Cupcake Cafe (#65).

EATS FOR KIDS The nearby strip of St. Marks Place was home-base for punk rockers, and it's lined with street vendors selling loud T-shirts and studded jewelry, but the vibe becomes mellower on the avenues. Take your pick between several sit-in or take out restaurants. Five-dollar falafel meals are a bargain at **Tahini** (23 3rd Ave., tel. 212/254–0300). You can grab a slice at **2 Brothers Pizza** (32 St. Marks Pl., 212/777–0600). Or try some crispy Belgian fries at **Pommes Frites** (123 2nd Ave., 212/674–1234), with 26 sauces to chose from. (Don't worry, ketchup is still an option.)

GREENWAY BIKE/WALKING PATH

Just as some see the legacy of Robert Moses as highways dividing and destroying communities, some think Bloomberg's legacy will be bicycle lanes and waterfront space reuniting the city's citizens with their green spaces.

The Greenway Path is the best of both initiatives. Part of a car-free biking path that is envisioned to one day stretch 2,500 miles from Maine to Florida, this 13-mile stretch begins near the southern point of Battery Park City and ends past Harlem all the way near Inwood Hill Park. That is pretty much the full length of Manhattan.

While few kids will do the whole path, there are points of interest all along it. Almost anywhere you begin or end will offer something for children. Here are the most interesting points, starting from the southernmost tip and ending at the Little Red Lighthouse.

Battery Park City: Someday this path may connect to its cousin on the east side. Until then, start here, where you can bike separate from the frantic NYC traffic. There's enough

EATS FOR KIDS The city developed its waterfronts and its eateries in tandem. In Battery Park City there are several restaurants ranging from fast food to fine dining. Still, we'd suggest you hold out for a picnic alfresco around Pier 54, Chelsea Piers, or Pier 84. If you can wait until then, the **Boat Basin Cafe** (W. 79th St., tel. 212/496–5542) turns out veggie burgers, basic salads, sandwiches, and other kid-faves.

Popular entrances include Battery Park City, Pier 84 (42nd), Clinton Cove (55th), and Riverside Park (70th–96th). All are along the Hudson River.

 Free; Bike rentals range from $8/hour (kid's bike), $34 for 4 hours (beach cruiser), to $69/day (tandems, racing bikes)

 All ages

here to keep kids busy for several hours, including the Irish Hunger Memorial, Wintergarden, Nelson Rockefeller Playground, and Tom Otterness sculptures.

Peddle past the West Village and stop at Pier 51's water playground. You may be lucky enough to catch a trapeze class in full swing. Biking past Midtown you can stop at the Dancing Fountain at Pier 84. All along the Upper West Side you'll be in Riverside Park, with several fun sculptures and a great outdoor restaurant, The Boat Basin Cafe. If you make it up to Harlem, the Riverbank State Park has a carousel and two playgrounds. Most people end their ride at "The Little Red Lighthouse and The Great Gray Bridge" (aka Jeffrey's Hook Light and The George Washington Bridge). During warmer months the Urban Rangers will periodically open the lighthouse for visitors.

If you like this sight, you may also like Central Park (#57).

MAKE THE MOST OF YOUR TIME

Bikes are available for rental at several places along the path. We suggest **Bike & Roll** (18 Battery Pl., tel. 212/509–0067) for the widest selection of family-friendly vehicles.

KEEP IN MIND Like everything in Manhattan, this path is filled with competitive, aggressive people. Fast bikers, messengers, and rushing pedestrians can make this an obstacle course even for seasoned riders. Teach your kids the basics in bike courtesy: how to signal turns or what it means when someone barks out, "On your left!"

GUGGENHEIM

45

I f the Met is Meryl Streep and the MoMA is Madonna, the Guggenheim is Audrey Hepburn.

Anywhere else, this collection of 7,000 "non-objective" (aka abstract) and impressionist artworks housed in a block-long spiral building—itself a masterpiece—would be a vibrant headliner. In NYC it's a demure leading lady, lovely and unassuming. It's lack of popularity with family visitors makes this doubly ironic, as it's arguably the world's most kid-friendly modern art museum.

For starters, the architecture. From the outside, kids see a giant white ribbon going around. From the inside it's a huge spiral ramp kids joyfully run down (or at least walk). Kids accustomed to the adult world's being very very square are immediately drawn to this rotunda. Download the Architecture Activity Guide from the museum's Web site to discover shapes used here rarely found in buildings (including hexagons, triangles, and teardrops).

KEEP IN MIND The museum very generously puts together an Activity Pack families can borrow to make the most of their visit. Go to the information desk to get the pack filled with artwork-specific question cards, touch objects, games, picture books, sketchpads, and pencils.

MAKE THE MOST OF YOUR TIME The main collection—with its whimsical Kandinskys and geometric Albers—is usually the most appealing part for kids (aside from walking down the spiral). Plan to spend at least half your time there. Fortunately, just as kids are ready for a bit of a break, you come to the **Cafe 3**. This little secret tucked away on the third floor overlooking Central Park is a great spot to recharge with a brownie.

Start out by taking the elevator to the top of the rotunda, then walk down the spiral, stopping off at floors along the way. The temporary exhibits, while often dealing with topics too sophisticated and abstract for the youngest minds, are almost always visually arresting enough to capture their attention. And if not, the joy of looking over the railing and up at the skylight is usually worth a good 20 minutes.

Then there's the scope. The permanent collection, housed in the Annex, is ultimately doable in an hour or less if need be. Since most of the paintings were done after the 1850s, we're talkin' bright colors, bold shapes, familiar subject matter. Marquee names like Klee, Chagall, Miro, Van Gogh, and Kandinsky line the walls. Finally, every weekend they run tours and drop-in art programs. The instructors really understand kids, and allow them the space for their free-form creativity to come through. While kids may not beg you to come back, they won't leave moaning either.

If you like this sight, you may also like the Museum of Modern Art (#33).

EATS FOR KIDS **The Wright restaurant** in the museum has an excellent lunch special. Adults get an appetizer and entrée, made from fresh local ingredients where possible, for $24. Kids can request a simple pasta with butter and Parmesan or marinara sauce, or modify one of the menu dishes.

HISTORIC RICHMOND TOWN

In the heart of Staten Island, this beautiful 100-acre park may be one of the city's best-kept secrets. The village contains 28 preserved historic buildings and a few reconstructions that interpret three centuries of Staten Island's daily life and culture. Ten buildings are on their original sites; the others were moved from elsewhere on Staten Island. Currently 12 buildings are open to the public.

The village of Richmond began in the 1690s as a crossroads settlement between scattered farms. The congregation of the Reformed Dutch Church built a combined religious meeting house, school, and residence for its lay minister and teacher around 1695. By 1730 Richmond had become the island's principal political center, and throughout the 18th century the village continued to increase in importance, acquiring a jail, courthouse, churches, taverns, and shops.

Begin at the 1837 Third County Courthouse Visitor Center to get a visitor's guide to points of interest. The Historical Museum is in the former County Clerk's Office. The Voorlezer's

MAKE THE MOST OF YOUR TIME If you're planning a visit, call to see if any special family events (reservations required for some) are coming up. This includes Halloween in Richmond Town, Old Home Day/Harvest Festival, Christmas in Richmond Town, an Independence Day Celebration, Pumpkin Picking at the Decker Farm, and a historic military Encampment Weekend. Kids 4–12 will be especially entertained. The Richmond County Fair also takes place here, combining traditional events with modern pastimes.

441 Clarke Ave., Staten Island

 $5 adults, $3.50 children 5–17 and students; $4 seniors

July–Aug, W–Su 11–5; Sept–June, W–Su 1–5; Tours W–F 2:30, Sa–Su 2 and 3:30

 718/351–1611; www.historicrichmondtown.org, www.richmondcountyfair.org

All ages

House is Richmond's oldest building on its original site, as well as the country's oldest elementary schoolhouse. Visitors of all ages marvel at demonstrations of printing, tinsmithing, and other trades performed by artisans in period costumes. Children 4–10 will enjoy these hands-on activities the most, and may be asked to lend a hand in the Basketmaker's House or help with another chore. When demonstrations aren't happening, a guide is present to give an overview of the setting and answer questions.

More than 200 of the best-loved toys from the 1840s to the present are displayed in the Historical Museum in TOYS!

If you like this sight, you may also like National Museum of the American Indian (#31).

EATS FOR KIDS
A picnic area is just east of the visitor center. Or try on-site **Bennett Cafe**, open for breakfast on Sundays, lunch on Thursday and Fridays, and dinner sporadically. The menu is extremely limited (2–4 items), but includes standard favorites like grilled cheese or pancakes.

KEEP IN MIND If you are traveling in a group with at least 10 kids (grades 3 through 6), you can book your own Mystery Murder and Mischief sleepover here. Families make their own candles, pop their own corn, churn butter, and uncover the "back story" of one of the most sensational murder trials in American history. In the very courtroom where Polly Bodine was tried for murder in 1834, they cuddle in their sleeping bags and participate in the dramatic retelling of Polly's mysterious and bizarre trial.

INTREPID SEA, AIR & SPACE MUSEUM

For many years this was a must-do for husbands, sons, and those with a proclivity for the military. But most moms just walked around with that glazed-over look you see when they're dragged to auto shows or comic-book conventions.

They've gone a long way toward rectifying this in recent years by adding narrative elements that make the experience more accessible to the less testosterone-laden members of the public.

Begin with the short film giving context to the aircraft carrier by sharing some of its history. Then grab an audio tour—listening to the actual pilots and crew members makes the steel and paint come to life. The tour will lead you around the inside of the vessel and take between 45 minutes and an hour.

KEEP IN MIND

Check first to make sure there is no major patriotic event taking place during your visit. The *Intrepid* is frequently closed or crowded for events like Veterans Day.

MAKE THE MOST OF YOUR TIME Get there as early as you can, as tours fill up quickly. This is an ideal stop during your Greenway bike trip, as there are plenty of bike racks and a big splash fountain for kids to play in.

Pier 86, 12th Ave. and 46th St.

 212/245-0072; www.
intrepidmuseum.org

 $22 adults; $17 children
3–17 and veterans; free
children under 3, US Active Military, Retired US
Military

 Apr–Oct, M–F 10–5, Sa and Su 10–6;
Nov–Mar, 10–5 daily; closed M

 5 and up

The biggest thrill for most visitors is, naturally, the planes on the deck. As it can get crowded, allow plenty of time to go around the 30 planes. Highlights include a walk through the Concorde (who knew it was that small inside?) and seeing the world's fastest plane (the A-12 Blackbird spy plane, which flies at 2,269 miles per hour).

If you like this sight, you may also like New York Transit Museum (#21).

EATS FOR KIDS If you are biking along the Greenway (#46), there are several good refueling spots along the path. If not, head to the **Sullivan Street Bakery** (533 W. 47th St.) about three blocks away. This bakery has a cult following for its Semi di Sesamo bread, amongst others. Flatbread pizzas are another good lunch-on-the-go. And save room for the bombolinis—outstanding Italian-style doughnuts.

JEWISH MUSEUM

42

The curators make this a kid-friendly place by taking objects and people representative of "the Jewish experience" and spinning them into a universal story, applicable to everyone regardless of religion, race, or nationality.

Take the recent exhibit, "Curious George Save the Day." Spotlighting not only many originals from the beloved books, it also shows how its Jewish authors (Margaret and H.A. Rey) escaped the Nazis thanks to the Curious George illustrations in their suitcases. Or the "Houdini: Art and Magic" exhibit, demonstrating how this Hungarian Jew and son of a rabbi went from a fledgling circus performer to the becoming the world's most famous magician. Although his secrets will not be revealed, many of his magic apparatus will be on display. Whenever you come, there is always at least one exhibit so evocative that children will momentarily forget they're in a museum.

The permanent exhibit, "Culture and Continuity: The Jewish Journey," has 800 objects showcasing international Jewish identity. While younger kids may not focus through the

MAKE THE MOST OF YOUR TIME Plan to spend at least 45 minutes at Archaeology Zone: Discovering Treasures from Playgrounds to Palaces. Here kids live the life of an archaeologist by interpreting symbols in a colorful mosaic, creating works of art inspired by objects in the Museum's collection, or dressing in costumes.

1109 5th Ave., at 92nd St.

 212/423-3200; www.
thejewishmuseum.org

 $12 adults, $7.50
students 13 and up,
$10 seniors, under
12 free, Sa free

 Su–T 11–5:45, Th 11–8, F 11–5:45, Sa
11–5:45 (Archaeology Zone is closed)

 2 and up

whole trip, its worth a quick visit. Young visitors tend to find the re-creation of an ancient synagogue of interest, where older children enjoy television and radio programs from the museum's broadcast archive, as well as a film on Jewish rituals in a gallery filled with ceremonial objects.

During the week there are several art and culture workshops for children of different ages. Most include a walk around the current kid-friendly exhibit and then a studio session to make art.

The museum is also one of the few open on Mondays (closed Saturdays).

If you like this sight, you may also like the Lower East Side Tenement Museum (#39).

KEEP IN MIND Around special events, both Jewish and non-Jewish holidays, there are family celebrations and themed happenings. For example, at Hanukkah kids can make their own glowing menorah using low-tech electronics.

EATS FOR KIDS Lunch, snacks, and a light dinner are available at the museum's glatt (that means ultimate) kosher Cafe Weissman. For something more novel, try the **Barking Dog Luncheonette** (1678 3rd Ave., tel. 212/831–1800), offering breakfast, lunch, dinner, and brunch. The puppy-themed decor entrances young ones, and a drinking fountain just for canines provides a constant dog parade. Try a burger on focaccia bread, meat loaf, or a yogurt sundae with granola topping.

KARMA KIDS YOGA

4

Welcome to the city's only yoga studio designed specifically for families. The passion founder Shari Vilchez-Blatt brings to her classes sets it apart from other yoga spots. Local families are such raving fans; it's common to see kids run up and hug her on the street.

Don't worry that the practice of yoga is too lofty for your little one. Teachers keep classes light and fun, using clever metaphors to engage kids. Rather than recite the adult names for the poses, kids are asked to imitate a cat chasing its tail or a jungle animal racing through the forest. There is plenty of movement in these classes; kids are both up and running around and also sitting doing poses.

The schedule is visiting-family friendly. Most classes are on a drop-in basis, you can go once or every day of your vacation without having the hassle of enrollment or pre-

MAKE THE MOST OF YOUR TIME

Reserve your spot in advance, at least by a few days (or a few hours in the summer). It's rare, but classes do fill up, and you don't want to risk being shut out.

EATS FOR KIDS The area around Union Square (2 blocks east) has several great options for a quick meal. Pick up picnic food at **Whole Foods** (4 Union Sq., tel. 212/673–5388) and eat it in the indoor seating area or head to the brand-new playground in Union Square Park. For a new twist on an old fave, stop in at **Dogmatic** (26 E. 17th St., tel. 212/414–0600). The food here's free of anything artificial. Sausages (beef, chicken, lamb, turkey) are put into fresh, hot baguettes and served with your choice of sauce like jalapeño or mint yogurt. Kids also enjoy the handmade sodas.

104 W. 14th St.

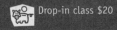 Drop-in class $20

 Class times vary

646/638-1444;
www.karmakidsyoga.com

All ages

registration. They do request that you call in advance to do a drop-in class, making it easier and faster for all concerned.

On most days there is at least one class for each age group: a prenatal class, Story Time Yoga (infant–6 years), Mommy & Baby for infants, Parent & Child for walkers through age 3, and Kids Yoga divided into groups by age (3- to 4-year-olds, 4–6, 7–9, 10–12, and teens).

In addition to the Village location, they run classes in TriBeCa, Brooklyn, Chelsea, and the Upper East Side.

If you like this sight, you may also like the beach at Rubin Museum (#12).

KEEP IN MIND Another organization, Circus Yoga (212/712–9644), offers community workshops teaching teachers how to make yoga more fun and effective by combining circus-like maneuvers with traditional yoga poses. In warmer months you will often find free, open-to-all events held in Central Park.

LIBERTY SCIENCE CENTER

Science and Sociology Center is more like it. Kids, and most adults, will love this science center's focus on application, not theory.

40

There are two animal exhibitions: "Eat and Be Eaten" and "Our Hudson Home," where children can see live animals and learn more about the adaptations used to avoid being eaten and to help capture prey. As they say here, poison, camouflage, hide and seek, and other weapons of warfare have been used in the natural world for far longer than human beings have been using them in the military one.

Little is more fun to a kid then seeing a real live parasite that can wipe out a city. In Infection Connection, be sure to leave time for actual lab work (lab hours are 10 AM–1 PM and 1:30 PM–4 PM), so kids can study and identify microbes and see how to protect themselves against disease.

In the Skyscraper! exhibit kids can get the inside view of how these urban giants are built through some interesting hands-on experiences, including stepping into a wind tunnel and

KEEP IN MIND This is a perfect complement to the New York Hall of Science, with its focus on deconstructing science from a kid's perspective (e.g., How does gravity work? Is a white light really white?). The center's main question is "How does this work?," focusing on the human interplay with science, answering "How do we impact science and how does science impact us?"

walking on a narrow steel beam 18 feet above the gallery floor without a net (but with a harness! Minimum height is 4 feet).

If your kid is still bouncing around, head to the outdoor Wildlife Challenge. Think ropes course from an insect's perspective. (Check in advance to make sure it's open.)

And that's just the first act. With an IMAX theater, live science demonstrations (with audience volunteers), 12 exhibitions, and sleepovers (winter only), this is well worth a PATH train ticket, especially on bad-weather days.

Don't miss climbing up to the Observation Deck (top floor) to snap a photo with clear views of Ellis Island, Manhattan, and the Statue of Liberty as a backdrop.

If you like this sight, you may also like the New York Hall of Science (#24).

EATS FOR KIDS

Check out the great views and a range of meals and snacks from soup to sandwiches at **Café Sky-lines**. Also, if you've brought your own bag lunch, ask at the welcome desk about indoor or outdoor spots to park your picnic.

MAKE THE MOST OF YOUR TIME Kids 6–15 will get the most out of their visit. Print out the age-appropriate official Liberty Science Center Scavenger Hunt from their Web site. Upon completion, they become "Scientist for a Day" and get a certificate. Visitors with children under 5 can also find online a section with tips just for them.

LOWER EAST SIDE TENEMENT MUSEUM

The tag line for this museum should be, "How to get your kids to stop grumbling about the shared bathroom!" Although the real goal here is giving kids an appreciation for immigrant life in America, the bonus is something much more practical, if less noble: serious ammo the next time they whine about sharing space with siblings.

Chronicling a variety of immigrant experiences in Manhattan's Lower East Side, this urban living–history museum is only accessible by joining one of six tours, each representing a different family's experience.

For example, the Confino family tour (5 and older) uses a costumed interpreter to share the joys and hardships of life in the tenement. This includes 10 people living in three rooms, all totaling less than the square footage of the average suburban garage; washing their hair on the fire escape; chasing rats out with a broom; and sharing a toilet with almost everyone in the building.

KEEP IN MIND

Tour tickets are available on a first-come, first-served basis, and they sell out quickly, as groups are limited to 15. Tickets for weekday tours and programs may be purchased in advance by credit card online or by calling 866/811–4111. Call the visitor center for details about multitour discounts on advance tickets.

MAKE THE MOST OF YOUR TIME
Make this your one day to do the Lower East Side. It's an ideal New York City neighborhood to explore from a historical perspective, because it's a classic mix of old–school immigrant shops and super hipster boutiques. Visit **Russ & Daughters** (179 E. Houston St., tel. 212/475–4880), a neighborhood institution since 1914, still serving killer babka, or **The Pickle Guys** (49 Essex St.) with 15+ varieties of pickles picked from barrels, and compare them to super-trendy shops like **Foley & Corinna** (114 Stanton St., tel. 212/529–2338) and **TG-170** (170 Ludlow St., tel. 212/995–8660), places tweens may appreciate.

Visitors Center, 108 Orchard St., at Delancey St.; tenement, 97 Orchard St.

 Tour $20 adults, $15 students and seniors

 Tour times vary between 11:15 and 5

212/982-8420; www.tenement.org

8 and up

But the tour also chronicles good times, too. The kids can play a real Victrola in the Confino's apartment and listen to the Confino's daughter tell stories about what she does in the few moments of free time she has—including going to Coney Island or the local Nickelodeon to see silent films.

The other tours tell the story of immigrants from Germany, Ireland, and Italy, but they're suggested for ages 8 and above, as there is no live actor to engage the children. The Irish family tour is suggested for ages 12 and up. Families with children 8 and up can also take the Next Steps neighborhood walking tour to get the backstory on the Lower East Side from 1935 to the present.

Recently the museum has started converting its second purchase, the building at 103 Orchard Street, into a Visitors Center housing exhibitions and classrooms.

If you like this sight, you may also like Ellis Island (#50).

EATS FOR KIDS The Lower East Side is a wonderland of kid-friendly delights specializing in the actual food immigrants ate back in the day. Get knishes (dough pockets like calzones) or potato latkes (pancakes) at **Yonah Schimmel's Knishery** (137 E. Houston St., tel. 212/477-2858), a Lower East Side institution that began from a pushcart. For dim sum or veggie dumplings, try the **Dumpling House** (118A Eldridge St., tel. 212/625-8008). Top it all off at **Economy Candy** (108 Rivington St., tel. 212/254-1531), a store packed floor to ceiling with virtually every candy that's ever been made.

MADAME TUSSAUDS WAX MUSEUM

Locals never step foot in here, perhaps because it's seen as a hokey tourist joint.

But don't let that jaded attitude stop you. There's plenty of silly fun to be had playing around the waxworks and snapping photos.

At Opening Night Party star-struck kids can impress their friends on Facebook by uploading their wild night in New York City with Angelina Jolie, the Osbournes, J. Lo, and Jennifer Aniston.

In the "Gallery" hobnob with the world's intellectual and political elite, including Ghandi, the Dalai Lama, Nelson Mandela, and the Pope. Take a picture in the Oval Office with President Obama.

Check out the Behind The Scenes, where kids can learn what it takes to make an ultra realistic wax figure from measurement to makeup. (Yes, each hair is put in individually.)

In recent years the museum has tried to expand its offerings by installing more interactive experiences. Two recommended ones are Cinema 4D (New York's only 4D theater, where kids

EATS FOR KIDS Times Square is filled with chain restaurants. If you are content with Appleby's, Red Lobster, or Chevy's, they are all within an easy one block. For a more local experience, grab falafel at **Maoz** (558 7th Ave., tel. 212/777–0820) to have a picnic at the tables in the Broadway Pedestrian Precinct. **Simply Pasta** (120 W. 41st St., tel. 212/391–0805) is one of the best values for a full-service restaurant. Penne alla Vodka, pasta primavera, and other Italian specialties are no more than $11.

234 W. 42nd St.

 $35.50 ages 13 and up, $28.50 children 4–12; free under 3, $32.50 seniors 60 and over

 10–10 daily

212/512-9600; www.NYCWAX.com

 5 and up

will not only experience a film in 3D action, they'll also feel wind, rain, and smell odors, making for an immersive experience), and Sports Zone (practice boxing or play with the Wii while wax sports stars watch).

Unless you're traveling with teens, avoid the one section completely inappropriate for children, SCREAM. It's filled with actors impersonating popular horror film characters.

Young moviegoers will recognize and enjoy the Pirates of the Caribbean Dead Man's Chest room, meant to replicate the famous Black Pearl Ship. Or see Superman Returns, housed in a giant dome theater intricately decorated like Metropolis. Children enter through a phone booth, and can pretend they're Superman as a subway car levitates in midair, inviting them to stand under and "lift" it.

If you like this sight, you may also like the Sony Wonder Technology Lab (#10).

MAKE THE MOST OF YOUR TIME
This is more like an exhibit than a whole museum. You follow a linear path through the displays, and backtracking isn't easy. Take photos, and take your time, with the "people" you encounter. You may never meet them again.

KEEP IN MIND It takes four months to create a wax figure, including 140 hours for artists to carefully insert hair strands one at a time. Many celebrities donate their clothes for their own figures. Joan Rivers even donated her favorite nail polish to make a perfect match. Once on exhibit, each wax portrait is inspected and groomed daily, and its hair is washed and makeup retouched regularly.

37

Sitting on top of Penn Station and spanning nearly 1 million square feet in the heart of New York City, this is perhaps the world's most famous arena. Generations of New Yorkers can fondly remember coming to "The Garden" to see a variety of sports, from boxing to basketball, as well as other types of performances. Today's Madison Square Garden traces its beginnings to the 1874 Great Roman Hippodrome, built by showman P.T. Barnum. In 1877 it was taken over by bandmaster Patrick Gilmore and renamed Gilmore's Garden. In 1879 Cornelius Vanderbilt's son, William, renamed the complex Madison Square Garden, and the title stuck with its descendant—which opened in 1968 and was fully renovated in 1991.

The main arena seats 20,000 and is the spring site of performances by Ringling Bros. and Barnum & Bailey Circus, a favorite of kids from preschoolers to teens. It's also home to the New York Knicks and New York Liberty basketball teams, New York Rangers hockey team, and events ranging from concerts to boxing bouts to dog shows. Your sports fans,

EATS FOR KIDS

Unlike the local baseball stadiums, food at MSG remains trapped in the land of greasy pizza and unnaturally neon nachos. For something more well-rounded, stop by **Lugo Caffé** (1 Penn Plaza, tel. 212/760–2700) pre-game, for eggplant caponata, Tuscan bean salad, or house-made pastas.

MAKE THE MOST OF YOUR TIME
Remember that Madison Square Garden is housed on top of Penn Station, a major transport hub. On weekdays during rush hour the streets around 7th Avenue in particular are incredibly congested, and it's rare to find a free cab. Factor in a little extra travel time and stick to the subway if you're getting out around 5 PM.

7th Ave. between 31 and 33rd Sts.

  Events vary

 212/465-MSG1, 212/465-5800
tours; www.thegarden.com

Varies by event;
tour 7 and up

young and old, will thoroughly enjoy a basketball or hockey game here any evening or afternoon. In 1877 Gilmore's Garden played host to the first annual N.Y. Bench Show, now known as the Westminster Kennel Club Dog Show. Various ice shows and other children's fare are offered throughout the year. The 5,600-seat WaMu Theater at Madison Square Garden also hosts children's shows, such as *Sesame Street Live* and most recently *Annie* and *Peter Pan*, as well as special events like the NFL draft. In the winter of 2007 the theater began hosting a brand-new Cirque du Soleil show, *Wintuk*, which will play for several years to come.

If you like this sight, you may also like a ballgame at Yankee Stadium (#1).

KEEP IN MIND The New York Liberty (New York's female basketball team) plays here. Tickets to their games can be the most affordable of any sport (starting at $10), although good seats are more in keeping with other sport prices ($20–$100). Stand by the entrance near 8th Avenue on the 33rd street side with an autograph book in hand. Many of your favorite sports stars enter this way, and are usually friendly about signing a book for kids.

METROPOLITAN MUSEUM OF ART

Claudia Kincaid, an 11-year-old New Yorker, feeling unappreciated, decides to run away from home. But the discomforts of runaway life aren't her style, so she decides to make the "Met" her new home.

Even kids who haven't read *The Mixed Up Files of Mrs. Basil E. Frankweiler* (required reading before a visit) can relate. This may be the Western Hemisphere's biggest museum, but if your kids are initiated the right way, they'll want to move right in, too.

Don't devote too much time to the painting galleries. Sure, there are plenty of old masters, new masters, paintings you didn't even know were masters, and you'll want to at least say you did it. But from a kid's point of view, the real treasures can't be hung on a wall. Instead, focus your time on these highlights before kids get museumed-out.

Egyptian Art: This may well be the best part of the visit. A chance to go into a real Egyptian temple (Temple of Dendur), plenty of mummies, coffins, cats, hieroglyphics, sphinxes, and William the Hippopotamus.

EATS FOR KIDS Staying in the museum for lunch makes it easier to resume your art afternoon. **The American Wing Café** is the best mix of casual atmosphere and refined food, and it offers a nice view. The self-serve **cafeteria** is for kids who will only eat chicken fingers or french fries. If you're ready to call it quits, head out to experience an old-fashioned soda jerk—one of the very few left in NYC—the **Lexington Candy Shop** (1226 Lexington Ave., tel. 212/288–0057). The milk shakes and malts are fun, even if the burgers and fries are unremarkable.

Equestrian Court & Hall of Arms: Let imaginations run wild as kids explore the castle-like courtyard with its knights riding brave steeds, both completely covered in shining armor.

American Wing: A giant atrium filled with fountains, sculpture, gaslights, and the entire facade of the Branch Bank of the United States that once stood at 15½ Wall Street. Off to the side are period rooms showing kids how families lived over the past few centuries (at least the wealthy ones!).

In summer the roof garden usually has something of interest to children, whether it's a 60-foot bamboo building kids could tour or Jeff Koons' gigantic Balloon Dog. And the entire family can appreciate the sweeping view.

If you like this sight, you may also like the Museum of Modern Art (#33).

MAKE THE MOST OF YOUR TIME

If you had three weeks to do nothing but this museum, you'd still find more to do. Have a frank discussion with your children about what you'll be covering on your trip, then reward them by going to the spots they will love.

KEEP IN MIND Preparing in advance for your visit will make it the more memorable. Visit the "Museum Kids" section on the Met's Web site. There you'll find family podcasts meant for 4- to 9-year-olds presenting small stories about one item or collection. Download several Family Guides and use them to plan what to see and when. The Explore & Learn activities are multimedia storybooks. Finally, the site lists in detail all family activities and programs available during your visit. Wait until you arrive to get the hard copy of The Family Map, it has a terrific "I Spy" game on the back.

MOOMAH

Think of this as multitasking at its most relaxing. Tracy Stewart (wife of comedian Jon Stewart) founded this café/arts and crafts and movement studio out of a desire to slow down and connect with her children.

The whole space exudes tranquillity, and it rubs off on children. The furnishings and decor—robin's-egg blue booths, overstuffed brown leather chairs, crafts projects housed in chicken-coop wire baskets—recall a gentler time and place. Staff members are patient and speak softly. But it isn't exactly sleepy here, there are plenty of activities that make this a great rainy-day stop.

The café is an excellent value, and it strikes the perfect balance between kid-friendly and refined, while dishing up cuisine that's fresh and healthy to boot. The star attraction is the Supertryer Sampler, which gives children a button if they taste any six of the food choices including bananas, tomatoes, green peas, avocado, dates, and more. Adults get Greek yogurt, pastries from Balthazar, sandwiches, smoothies, even a glass of wine if they want.

MAKE THE MOST OF YOUR TIME

Moomah is closed on Sundays for private events. It also occasionally closes over weekend holidays when locals are often out of town, so check the Web site for opening hours.

EATS FOR KIDS At least half the appeal of Moomah is the food, and you'll be hard-pressed to find a lunch spot that caters to kids more, so if you're coming here for the arts and crafts, don't leave without at least stopping by the café for a little "frog dipper" (guacamole and chips dressed up to look like a smiling frog face).

In a sunny craft room, low tables are set up for little hands and staff members are quick to step over and assist. It all begins with a DIT kit (Do-It-Together). While slightly pricy (averaging about $12), kits are well done, with nature themes like an "On The Shore" placemat or "A Bug's Life" shadowbox. Projects require just a little gluing and stringing, not a Martha Stewart–level fastidiousness.

The back room ("Funky Forest") seems abstract in concept: an interactive space where children's movements influence the "health" of an electronic "ecosystem." But once kids begin to jump and dance around in front of the LCD screen, and the projected images of aquatic life begin to move in response, there's no explanation needed.

If you like this sight, you may also like The Art Farm in the City (#66).

KEEP IN MIND In addition to drop-in crafts, they also offer long-term art and nature classes for kids (usually season long) and visiting artist events for adults. Make a half day of it by combining your visit here with a meal from the café. It's a great way to save some time and enjoy a healthy meal.

MOVIES FOR KIDS

Gone are the days when being a cineaste was restricted to the over-21 set. Tech-savvy kids armed with iPhones and weaned on YouTube are getting into movie-watching and movie-making in droves. New York City, the East Coast's film hub, had been slow coming to the game. But with Robert DeNiro's founding of the Tribeca Film Festival, the city is making up for lost time with a ton of opportunities.

For starters, the Tribeca Film Festival itself periodically runs films for kids, so check their Web site (www.tribecafilm.com/news-features/family). Usually on the first Saturday of the festival (around May 1st) they have an all-out outdoor extravaganza (the Family Festival). Entirely free, it is the city's most exciting street festival, with numerous neighborhood and film-related activities, performances, freebies, and community outreach booths.

The International Children's Film Festival (www.gkids.com), usually held in winter, is a 2- to 3-week-long spotlight of the best animated and non-animated films for children. Typically screenings take place around various theaters, including Symphony Space (#6)

KEEP IN MIND There is no dearth of museums dedicated to film and television in the city. In Queens the Museum of the Moving Image (3601 35th Ave., Queens, tel. 718/784–0077) recently underwent a complete renovation. Now it's a powerhouse of film-related exhibits, classes, lectures, and screenings. At the Paley Center (25 W. 52nd St., tel. 212/621–6600) families can pick from 150,000 TV shows and advertisements. Chances are you'll find ones that haven't been posted on YouTube yet. MoMA regularly runs weekend short thematic films for kids that are usually tied to the arts.

Multiple venues

 www.tribecafilm.com, www.gkids.com,
www.bryantpark.org, www.riversideparkfund.org,
www.hudsonriverpark.org, www.centralparknyc.org

 Prices vary by screening

 All ages

and the IFC (323 6th Ave., tel. 212/924–7771). Tickets are affordable, usually ranging $8–$14, and the films are ones you will almost certainly never see anywhere else, Netflix or otherwise.

During the summer there are at least 10 different outdoor film festivals dotted around the five boroughs showing family-friendly classics and recent releases, like *The Wizard of Oz* and *Up*. It's become a tradition for families to picnic on blankets under the stars before the movie. The most popular festivals are Bryant Park Summer Film Festival (www.bryantpark.org), Riverside Park's Movies Under the Stars (www.riversideparkfund.org), RiverFlicks for Kids (www.hudsonriverpark.org), and ending the summer on a sweet note, the Central Park Conservancy Film Festival (www.centralparknyc.org).

If you like this, you may also like Broadway on a Budget (#64).

MAKE THE MOST OF YOUR TIME
Advance booking is absolutely crucial for almost all events except the summer film festivals—in which case you should get there at least an hour early to stake out the best seats.

EATS FOR KIDS For a truly thematic experience, eat at the **Cinema Café** (505 3rd Ave., tel. 212/689–9022). A silent film plays while families eat bistro/trattoria specialties like bacon-wrapped turkey sliders, handmade pastas, Neapolitan pizzas, and coconut shrimp.

MUSEUM OF MODERN ART

This place divides into two camps: "Yay!" or "Yawn."

Whether the Museum of Modern Art, aka the MoMA, is sheer delight or pure torture for kids depends on your planning skills, current exhibits, and when you go. The MoMA tries to pull kids into modern art from the cradle. Recent initiatives have reinforced their mission: they've added kids' audio tours, expanded family programming, added an indoor drop-in "shape lab," and made several downloadable gallery guides on their Web site.

Begin with most kid-friendly exhibits. In recent years MoMA has pushed its populism by doing at least one temporary installation with wide appeal. Galleries displaying Tim Burton's madcapped creations like fluorescent spinning tops, cartoons, and costumes from his movies were a big hit with kids.

Sculpture, especially modern art with its tactile tentacles, oversize body parts, and strange placement—a bicycle wheel growing out of a stool?—is also a fun stop. Since it shares

KEEP IN MIND

MoMA's gift shops are two of the best in the city, well worth the splurge. Here you'll find everyday objects with an aesthetic twist, funky kids toys, and a fun selection of artistic picture books.

MAKE THE MOST OF YOUR TIME

Before you go, check out the excellent "Planning Your Visit with a Family" section of their Web site. It's fairly comprehensive, and includes helpful recommendations like how long to visit with a child (30–90 minutes) or the least crowded times to go (morning, weekdays). Upon arrival, pick up the MoMA Audio: Modern Kids audio program and a gallery guide at the Education and Family Information Desk. At best, these extend a kid's tolerance.

gallery space with the paintings, adults can glimpse famous modernists like Klee, Matisse, and Picasso while kids gaze at the a real helicopter overhead. (Yes, this is another "sculpture.")

If you can handle the crowds, go on a weekend to experience the extensive family programming. Every Saturday and Sunday there are drop-in Tours for Fours and A Closer Look for Kids workshops. Tour leaders follow a theme as they take families to 4–5 works in the gallery. At each piece there is a discussion paired with a small art project. In the theater at noon they screen short family-friendly films you won't see elsewhere—they all have artistic themes and there is usually a discussion in between. Both programs are free with admission. For children 7 and under, the ground-level shape lab allows kids to play with shapes in different media (computers, magnetic Colorforms, furniture, blocks).

If you like this sight, you may also like the Guggenheim (#45).

EATS FOR KIDS Cafe 2 is such a good value for kids. For $6, children get handmade pasta in butter or a fresh marinara sauce, and it's big enough for siblings to share. Adult meals are slightly more (approx. $11) but with options like artisanal cheese plates, wild-mushroom tart, and pan-seared salmon, it's still a good value. Super-fast service, plentiful seating, and a buzzing environment that will support any loud child chatter makes this a Midtown best bet.

Kids like this museum because it chronicles their everyday life. The collections are filled with tangible items they can relate to.

Both this and its cousin on Central Park West (the New-York Historical Society) exist primarily to codify New York City. But, where the historical society approaches history from a personality and political angle, this museum is focued on daily life.

Plenty of the museum's 1.5 million-plus items spanning 400 years of NYC history appeal to kids. Show them seats from the original Yankee Stadium, a 1980 Checker cab, a piece of the old mechanical Times Square news "zipper," or a giant bolt tightener used to build the Brooklyn Bridge.

New York Toy Stories is another must-see, including antique dolls and the famed Stettheimer Dollhouses, with original miniatures of great 20th-century works of art.

EATS FOR KIDS One perk of the NYC melting pot culture is the glorious range of cuisine. Try something new at **Lechonera El Barrio** (172 E. 103rd St., tel. 212/722–1344). Adults can experiment with Puerto Rican specialties like *relleno de papa, mofongo de pollo,* and *batido de mamey.* Less adventurous kids can always fall back on rice and beans.

1220 5th Ave., at 103rd St.

 Suggested donation $20 families, $10 adults, $6 students, free 12 and under

212/534-1672; www.mcny.org

 T–Su 10–5

4 and up

On Saturdays once a month there is a family program thematically connected to an exhibit—usually an art project or performance. Recent ones included choreographed sword fighting (no interactivity in that one) and Japanese fan making tied to the "Samurai in New York" exhibit.

The theater collection includes artifacts codifying the Broadway experience, like costumes, sets, posters, and drawings.

If you like this sight, you may also like the New-York Historical Society (#23).

KEEP IN MIND
At PROTECT! kids learn how fire and fire safety have shaped the Big Apple over four centuries by seeing bucket brigades, hose carriages, and pumpers that were pulled not by horses but by firefighters.

MAKE THE MOST OF YOUR TIME Get context by first watching the film *Timescapes: A Multi-Media Portrait of New York* projected on three screens in a specially designed theater (every half-hour beginning from 10:15–4:15). It documents more than four centuries of the city's development from its origins as a tiny settlement of Native Americans, Europeans, Dutch traders, and enslaved Africans and African-Americans to today's megopolis.

NATIONAL MUSEUM OF THE AMERICAN INDIAN

Manhattan for $24?

This Dutch "bargain" was no more legit than buying an iPad that "fell off the truck." Native Americans, lacking the same land ownership beliefs as European explorers, were really just offering to share use of the land.

Beyond appealing to children's natural curiosity about other cultures, this NYC branch of the Washington DC Smithsonian Institution clears up this and other misconceptions about Native Americans, largely through personal interaction.

As part of the Institution's mission to empower the Indian voice, there are more live family-friendly programs than almost any NYC museum, and that's the main reason to come here.

Throughout the year kids can meet Native Americans across nations and tribes through dances, hands-on workshops, concerts, and storytelling programs. These participation-

KEEP IN MIND

Popular annual events include a Children's Festival, a Summer Dance program (two dance performances daily throughout July), the concert series Native Sounds Downtown, and the annual two-day celebration of the Latin American festival, Day of the Dead, around Halloween.

MAKE THE MOST OF YOUR TIME

As there are really only two places to take kids (the permanent exhibit and the Resource Center), this museum can easily be done in an hour or less. Consider passing through on your way to the Statue of Liberty or other points of interest downtown (its free, so there's nothing to lose if you breeze through quickly).

George Gustav Heye Center, 1 Bowling Green

 212/514-3700; www.americanindian.si.edu; for background, visit the museum blog: http://blog.nmai.si.edu

 Free

10–5 daily, Th until 8, closed only Dec 25

5 and up

heavy programs encourage children to ask questions and learn about native beliefs, history, legends, and lifestyle.

Visitors with younger children start at the Resource Center, a family-friendly room filled with materials to make the visit more enjoyable and give it context. Kids love to play with the computers loaded with interactive exhibits (these can be accessed at home as well), do the art projects, and read picture books. Often there are cultural interpreters on hand.

Children also enjoy browsing the museum's only permanent exhibit, Infinity of Nations, because the majority of objects were made for everyday use, of familiar materials, and have an animal theme. Allow 30–45 minutes to walk around the two floors looking at carved animal figures, elaborate clothes, feathers, baskets, and painted hides. Adults, be sure to look up at the frescoes painted on the rotunda wall. The neoclassical building itself is impressive and the interior even more so.

If you like this sight, you may also like the American Museum of Natural History (#67).

EATS FOR KIDS Pick up salad-bar food (sandwiches, salads, or soups) at **Zaytuna** (17 Battery Pl., tel. 212/871–6300), a few blocks from the museum. Take it to Battery Park across the street, and enjoy a picnic overlooking the water. Stone Street, a few blocks away, is considered this area's restaurant row,\ with several sit-down options. Try **Adrienne's Pizza Bar** (54 Stone St., tel. 212/248–3838) to sample their delicious rectangular pizza.

NBC STUDIOS TOUR

Television fans must take this tour. Although you won't see any stars, you'll get a behind-the-scenes tour of one of American's most powerful networks.

You'll start back in time with NBC's birth in the Golden Age of Radio. Then you'll visit the saccharine '40s and '50s shows your parents may have grown up on. At last, you'll be taken into 1 to 3 studios where they currently film popular shows like "Saturday Night Live," "Late Night with Jimmy Fallon," "NBC Nightly News," the "Today Show," and "Football Night in America." You can also learn about the latest TV technology used to broadcast around the world.

Purchase tickets in advance to guarantee your preferred day and time. Because so many groups book ahead of time, if you do choose to purchase your tickets on the day of your tour, you'll need to get here early. Tours are often sold out by early afternoon.

MAKE THE MOST OF YOUR TIME Schedule a "Rockefeller Center Day." This area of the city has a high concentration of kid-friendly attractions. You can combine this tour with a visit to Top of the Rock, Radio City Music Hall, the Rockefeller Center Ice Rink, or the windows of Saks Fifth Avenue (during holiday time). Start early, so you'll have plenty of energy!

NBC has been offering these tours since 1933. And even if you don't rub shoulders with a present-day NBC celebrity, you might be led around by a future one: an NBC page serves as your guide, and former pages have included Ted Koppel, Willard Scott, Regis Philbin, Steve Allen, Kate Jackson, and Michael Eisner.

If you like this sight, you may also like the behind-the-scenes tour at Radio City Music Hall (#14).

KEEP IN MIND

Check www.nbcstudiotour.com before you plan your visit to see if celebrity signings, special events, or new products will be unveiled on the day of your tour.

EATS FOR KIDS At the **Rock Center Café** (20 W. 50th St., tel. 212/332-7620), ask for a seat overlooking the skating rink in winter, the garden in spring/summer. Sports fans like **Mickey Mantle's** (42 Central Park S, tel. 212/688-7777) for its large portions, friendly service, oversize TV screens, and baseball memorabilia. **Prime Burger** (5 E. 51st St., tel. 212/759-4729) serves up filling burgers, shakes, and pies.

NEW VICTORY THEATER

Once the house lights dim there's no way you'll confuse this theater with the Disney one across the street. Any umbrella-toting nannies or under-sea princesses appearing on this stage are either going to be shadow puppets or Shakespearean sprites.

The New Victory staff travels the globe, literally, to find thought-provoking, edgy productions transcending traditional tropes, roles, and plots. The theater itself had a racy history as Broadway's first burlesque house in 1933, and then, in the '70s, Times Square's first XXX theater. But all that's history, and these days it's New York's preeminent venue for intelligent, sophisticated performances for the under-18 crowd. Although adults often enjoy it as much as the kids do. The ultra-reasonable prices make them happy, too—rarely is a ticket above $35—a real steal compared to Broadway musicals—and if it's part of a subscription it can even come close to half that.

Recent productions have included *Nevermore,* a surrealistic recounting of events shaping Edgar Allan Poe's life (11 and up); *Squirm Burpee Circus,* a vaudeville pandemonium

KEEP IN MIND The family workshops accompanying most of the shows sell out almost immediately. Try to get on the e-mail list to be notified when registration is open.

MAKE THE MOST OF YOUR TIME Visiting the Web site before booking is a must-do. Every single performance page has a directory of features to help you decide if a show is right for your kids: a video, short summary, and show dates; matrix with all the relevant info shown at a glance (e.g., age, length, narrative type, etc.).

(all ages); *Puss in Boots*, an opera puppet show (8 and up); and *Zoo Zoo*, featuring dancers so skilled that you'll forget they aren't the animals they're portraying.

Performances usually have corresponding workshops ($17), where children become acquainted with what they are going to see by practicing a few of the skills the performers themselves will do on stage. For example, performing vaudeville acts, learning hip-hop moves, or bringing puppets to life. Workshops sell out quickly, so reserve them in advance. There are also often same-day pre-show activities in the lower lobby—usually an art or movement project, all free.

Most shows run between two and six weeks, and have a run time of less than two hours. Booster seats are available.

If you like this site, you may also like Puppetworks (#17).

EATS FOR KIDS **Junior's** (W. 45th St., tel. 212/302–2000) is one of the few tourist-oriented restaurants in Times Square well worth a visit. Although the prices are somewhat outrageous and the food is merely decent, the cheesecake is the stuff of NYC legend. And the atmosphere is just as worthwhile—it hasn't changed much since the '50s, when it opened. (OK, the original location was in Brooklyn, but the spirit's the same.)

NEW YORK AQUARIUM

With its peeling paint, '60s architecture, and ocean-spray-rusted railings, the uninitiated would think this pales in comparison to the ultra-luxe modern marine mansions such as the Monterey Bay Aquarium or the Georgia Aquarium.

To devotees, however, this is just another part of the nostalgic charm representing an era of aquariums before corporate sponsorship. The new "Sea Change" initiative should hopefully update the facilities for a better user experience without eliminating the area's essence. Improvements will include a "re-imagined" aquatheater, a gigantic ocean tank with a shark exhibit, and family programs tying the aquarium to the ocean and modernizing its facilities.

Until then, this aquarium can hold its head high as home to more than 10,000 species of marine life, including Pacific walruses, giant sea turtles, sand-tiger sharks, and sea otters.

The sea lion show—where these magnificent animals show off their dexterity and jumping skills—doesn't lose its wonder, even after repeat viewings. In summer it can be blazingly

MAKE THE MOST OF YOUR TIME Taking a subway (N or D are best from Manhattan) is the fastest, cheapest, and safest way to get here. Only an hour from Manhattan, with departures almost every 10 minutes or more frequently, it beats the $20 parking fee and battling traffic. Get off at Stillwell Avenue, or West 8th if you take the F or Q train.

Boardwalk at W. 8th St.,
Coney Island, Brooklyn

$13 adults, $9 children
3–12, $10 seniors

718/265-FISH;
www.NYAquarium.com

May–Sept 6, 10–6 weekdays, 10–7 weekends
and holidays, Sept 7–Oct, 10–5 weekdays,
10–5:30 weekends; Nov–Apr, 10–4:30 daily

All ages

hot in the 1,600-seat Aquatheater, so either sit close to get splashed or sit on the top deck to use an umbrella. (Either way, slather kids in sunscreen.)

Alien Stingers comes in second in this popularity contest. The almost surreal vision of fluorescent balloons with ethereal tentacles against the blue of the ocean deep makes this a treat for adults as well.

Now it's on to the ever-popular predators: the 90,000-gallon tank holds sharks, turtles, fish, and stingrays. Be sure to ask why the sharks don't eat their fellow roommates.

In Explore the Shore your family can stand under a 400-gallon tidal wave that crashes every 30 seconds. A Plexiglas hood keeps you dry, but the power of the sea may leave you breathless.

If you like this sight, you may also like the Bronx Zoo (#63).

KEEP IN MIND
In summer, earn one of those "Mom/Dad, you're THE BEST!" hugs by combining this with a few hours at the brand-new Luna Park amusement park in Coney Island. Together they'll result in kids who'll sleep the whole subway ride home.

EATS FOR KIDS Assuming you didn't bring a picnic lunch (you can BYO picnic basket at tables in the aquarium), don't want food at the indoor Seaside Cafe, and can resist the siren song of Coney Island's crinkle fries at **Nathan's** (1310 Surf Ave., tel. 718/946–2202), expand your experience with lunch in Brighton Beach. Restaurants like **Tatiana** (3152 Brighton 6th St., tel. 718/891–5151) share the neighborhood's Russian flavor. With an opulent over-the-top dining room and 20-page menu, kids are sure to find a few things they like.

NEW YORK BOTANICAL GARDEN

Kids don't get jazzed about plants or spend time dissecting the difference between a Japanese maple and ashleaf maple.

And the NYBG knows that. They win kids over with attractions ranging from 10-minutes-of-distraction-so-you-take-a-quick-glance-at-those-orchids to hour-long nature retreats.

The latter include the wildly popular Holiday Train Show (end November–New Year's Day). Families go inside the Enid A. Haupt Conservatory (greenhouse) to follow the path of a train traveling around a mini–New York City including a model of Ellis Island, the Statue of Liberty, and Radio City Music Hall. Avoid crowds by going early in the day on a school day. Otherwise, prepare to spend at least an hour standing while filing through the exhibit.

MAKE THE MOST OF YOUR TIME

The botanical garden is less crowded on weekdays, except Wednesday, when admission is free (admission is also free Saturday 10 AM to noon). A narrated tram tour lets you explore various places then reboard. Guided walking tours and audio tours are best suited to older children.

The former is the Everett Children's Adventure Garden. Good for 45–90 minutes, it's a magical garden full of mazes, larger-than-life flowers, water plants, and an indoor laboratory.

EATS FOR KIDS The indoor–outdoor Garden Cafe and the Leon Levy Visitor Center Cafe serve kid-oriented comfort foods. Picnic tables are available at the Clay Family Picnic Pavilions, outside the Everett Children's Adventure Garden. Outside the garden, in Belmont, also called Arthur Avenue, try one of the many pizza parlors and Italian restaurants. **Dominick's** (2335 Arthur Ave., tel. 718/733–2807) and **Emilia's** (2331 Arthur Ave., tel. 718/367–5915) have inexpensive family-style Italian.

200th St. and Kazimiroff Blvd., Bronx

 T–Su, 10–6

 $6 adults, $3 students and seniors, $1 children 2–12; Sa 10–12 and all day W free

718/817–8700; www.nybg.org

1 and up

Check out the daily schedule of children's activities. There's usually one activity around growing, gardening, harvesting, or cooking aimed at children.

If you can secure some adult time, explore the magnificent 250 acres filled with 30,000 trees and 50 diverse gardens. A visit during spring and summer requires careful planning to ensure that you can see at least 4–5 of your favorite areas, since all are in bloom: orchids, lilacs, tulips, the herb garden, and flowering cherry trees. A fall visit is so magnificent it practically substitutes for an upstate drive.

In addition to the train show, there are several seasonal festivals. The Cherry Blossom Festival is a welcome end to winter (spring), the Edible Garden (summer and early fall) celebrates locally grown foods, and the Train Show (winter) brings the festivities of the holiday season. Booking in advance is advised.

If you like this sight, you may also like the Brooklyn Botanic Garden (#62).

KEEP IN MIND For a wonderful selection of gardening tools, toys, and plant-related items for children, visit The Kids Shop in the Children's Adventure Garden. The Gift Shop in the main retail area is also the place to take home a pint-sized pot for your child to plant at home. Consider bringing home a "please touch" plant for your garden. Lamb's ears, bee balm, lavender, and lemon balm all provide interesting textures, and the latter three are also aromatic when a child rubs its leaves.

In a renovated three-story firehouse built in 1904, you and your family can view one of the most comprehensive collections of fire-related art and artifacts from the 18th century to the present. Large firehouse doors, the housewatch (front desk) entrance, stone floor, brass sliding pole, and hose tower remind visitors of the former home of Engine Company 30, its firefighters, rigs, and horses. The nonprofit museum operates in partnership with the New York City Fire Department, which owns the building and provides the collection. Kids 5 and up may be captivated by the firefighters who serve as tour guides.

Highlights for young children or future firefighters include getting a picture taken in a real NYC fireman's helmet and coat. Young ones will also enjoy spotting "Chief," the firehouse canine hero tucked away in his corner. Grandparents, parents, and older children interested in fire memorabilia will all enjoy the toy and model exhibit on the second floor. Permanent and temporary exhibitions chronicle the evolution of fire-fighting technology, beginning with the early bucket brigades. Carefully preserved hand-operated, horse-drawn, and

EATS FOR KIDS Made with kids in mind, Moomah (#35) provides wholesome, organic eats in a café decked out with tabletop toys and cheerful artwork. The restaurant is just one branch of Moomah's mission. They also host craft classes ($12) and playtime to their trippy, illuminated "Funky Forest." **Bubby's** (120 Hudson St., tel. 212/219–0666) is a popular brunch spot with locals. Oversize muffins and sweet pancakes are kids' favorites, as are the board games available to while away the wait time.

278 Spring St., between
Hudson and Varick

 Suggested donation $7 adults,
$5 students

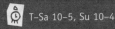 T–Sa 10–5, Su 10–4

 212/691–1303;
www.nycfiremuseum.org

2–and up

motorized equipment; toys; models; fire-engine lamps; presentation silver; oil paintings, prints, and photographs; "fire marks"; and folk art illuminate the traditions and lore of firefighting.

Preschoolers and early schoolers can learn why fires were a big problem in olden days and how bucket brigades worked. They'll be fascinated by how men pulled and pumped the early fire engines and how horses and dogs helped. They may also discover how firefighting changed as New York grew from a small village to a large city. Older kids can learn the evolution of fire alarms, the duties of today's firefighters, and the teamwork involved in fighting fires. Don't forget to ask the guides how Dalmatian dogs became associated with firefighting.

If you like this sight, you may also like the New York City Police Museum (#25).

MAKE THE MOST OF YOUR TIME

The building can get crowded when group tours arrive, so call ahead to see whether schools are scheduled when you're planning to visit.

KEEP IN MIND If you're looking for a real climb-on experience, you're better off at the New York City Transit Museum (#21). The fire trucks here are museum pieces, and exhibitions don't double as a hands-on playspace. Let your kids know what to expect.

NEW YORK CITY POLICE MUSEUM

Where else can you lock your kids in jail, let them play with guns, take them for a spin in a police cruiser, and help them fraternize with notorious criminals without someone calling Child Protective Services?

Actually, the guns are behind glass, there's no climbing on the cars, and the criminals are only in photos. But the spirit of Cops & Robbers make-believe is very much alive here, especially when kids climb inside an actual jail cell.

Start with the collection of vehicles on the first floor: a police cruiser, two motorcycles, bicycles, and a few scooters. Summer visitors should try to plan around the annual car show with 50+ classic patrol cars from all 50 states—including Starsky & Hutch's Ford Grand Torino.

To the Facebook generation, the adjacent telecommunications section can be quaint, with a switchboard, pre-rotary dial phones, even a telegraph. After doing police uniforms, go to the second-floor favorite, "Vintage Weapons & Notorious Criminals." Meet

KEEP IN MIND The museum's staff is a font of fun trivia. Ask nicely, and they'll share with you the answers to such puzzlers as, Why are police called cops? Who designed the Medal of Valor? Where can the Yankees logo be found in the museum and why?

MAKE THE MOST OF YOUR TIME The museum can be done quickly in 30–90 minutes, depending on your kid's attachment to law enforcement. The Hall of Heroes is the museum's most solemn room, containing the shields of every NYPD officer killed in the line of duty since the department began in 1845.

100 Old Slip (between
Water and South Sts.)

 212/480–3100;
www.nycpolicemuseum.org

 Suggested donation $7 adults,
$5 students, seniors and children,
free under 2 and members of service,

 M–Sa 10–5

 8 and up

America's favorite villains, from Benjamin "Bugsy" Siegel to Louise the Lump. The weapons include Al Capone's famous Tommy Gun.

There is a gift shop on the ground floor with plenty of kid-pleasing items, but one of the best souvenirs is a photo of your child in the real jail cell with the door closed (don't worry, there's no lock).

The top floor is dedicated to the permanent exhibit "9/11 Remembered"—simultaneously a tribute to those who helped and a disturbing reminder of the images and artifacts of destruction.

There are several annual events, often tied to holidays, where children can meet police officers, try on uniforms, and try out their detective skills. Particularly memorable are the annual Halloween Party and Junior Detective Day. Check the calendar for specifics.

If you like this sight, you may also like the New York City Fire Museum (#26).

EATS FOR KIDS For pub-style food, try **Stone Street Tavern** (52 Stone St., tel. 212/785–5658). The miniburgers at **Ulysses'** (95 Pearl St., tel. 212/482–0406) draw families and Wall St. financiers alike. Or head to **Adrienne's Pizza Bar** (54 Stone St., tel. 212/248–3838) for cheesy slabs of rectangle pizzas.

NEW YORK HALL OF SCIENCE

The assumption here is that every child is born a scientist. The mission is merely to grow knowledge and keep the fires of curiosity burning bright.

And certainly this institution succeeds in making the basic principles of science easy and entertaining. Although kids 7+ will get the most out of the entire facility, there is plenty to keep younger ones busy for a couple of hours.

For younger kids, start at Preschool Place. This indoor playspace includes a two-story magical treehouse hideaway with regular shows and story times. There is plenty for young hands to safely do here: make block buildings, stage a puppet show, turn cranks. Best of all, there is a staff member blocking entry at all times, giving toddler-toting parents a moment's respite.

Older kids will love almost everything here. Sports Challenge burns up their excess energy. In the Balance, Bounce, Climbing, Leap, Pitching, and Race challenges, kids do a fitness activity that demonstrates a principle of physics. Scale a real 8-foot climbing wall (learning

EATS FOR KIDS The on-site café has plenty of seats and a nice view of the playground, but the food is your typical dismal heat-lamp fare. A better option is **Corona Pizza** (5123 108th St., tel. 718/271–3736), a few blocks away. The slices here aren't brick-oven gourmet, but they're filling. More importantly, you'll be across the street from the **Lemon Ice King of Corona** (52–02 108th St., tel. 718/699–5133), a true Queens classic. Even in winter, kids get Italian ices in 30+ varieties as well as candy apples and other treats.

47–01 111th St., Flushing Meadows–Corona Park, Flushing, Queens

 $11 adults, $8 children 2–17, students and seniors

 July–Aug, M–F 9:30–5, Sa–Su 10–6; Sept–Mar, Tu–Th 9:30–2, F 9:30–5, Sa and Su 10–6; Apr–June, M–Th 9:30–2, Fri 9:30–5 PM, Sa and Su 10 AM–6 PM

 718/699-0005; www.nyscience.org

 2 and up, Science Playground all ages

about levers), throwing a fast ball (speed, trajectory, spin), surf on a real board (center of gravity).

As energy wanes and concentration grows, attend one of the demos or shows, or do experiments on one of 12 microscopes at the biochemistry or astronomy discovery lab. "Seeing the Light" centers on the world of color, light, and perception with 80+ exhibits. Discover how the eye works, appear to fly via an anti-gravity mirror, or shrink and grow by walking across the Distorted Room.

In summer, going to the Science Playground (30,000 square feet of water, sand, slide, and science goodness) is a must. Unfortunately, they have a policy of only allowing people to do 90-minute sessions—keep that in mind with younger kids.

If you like this sight, you may also like the Liberty Science Center (#40).

MAKE THE MOST OF YOUR TIME

The Queens location makes it mercifully immune to the crowds Manhattan museums are plagued with. Even during the busiest times, the only real wait you'll experience is for the outdoor playground. This makes it an ideal escape from Christmas crowds and holiday hordes.

KEEP IN MIND Students with 90% and above in both math and science can receive a free one-year Honors Membership to the museum, just another reason to hit the books. As for history, the Hall of Science is in Flushing Meadows–Corona Park, site of the 1939 and 1964 World's Fairs (its Unisphere is easily spotted from miles around). Also in the park are the Queens Zoo (tel. 718/271–1500) and the Queens Museum of Art (tel. 718/592–9700).

NEW-YORK HISTORICAL SOCIETY

New Yorkers believe their city is the center of the universe, and this museum only reinforces the argument. This cousin to the Museum of the City of New York across the park aims to show not only a slice of life through objects, it also strives to demonstrate just how far the city's influence reaches.

The rotating exhibits demonstrate this the most clearly. They don't focus solely on possessions or people with an obvious connection to New York City. They focus instead on topics, people, or events whose lives or outcomes were influenced by their connections to New York City. Two recent ones (Grateful Dead and Lincoln) show the city's role in each subject's popular and political ascent, respectively. But far from stuffy, both exhibits are easy to digest in a 10-minute walkthrough.

KEEP IN MIND The gift shop has many New York–themed items that make one-of-a-kind, reasonably priced souvenirs.

MAKE THE MOST OF YOUR TIME Do not pass go. Do not collect $200. Do not do anything but go directly to the brand-new Children's Center. Far more than a discovery room, this is a remarkable interactive opportunity for children to "meet" the famous figures from the past as children. It's a great way to experience history at a level kids can understand.

Of the 1.6 million items, here are some kid-friendly highlights: hundreds of toys, dolls, games, soldiers, and trains; the nation's largest collection of Tiffany glasswork; original watercolors from John J. Audubon's *Birds of America*; George Washington's camp bed from Valley Forge; and the desk where Clement Clark Moore wrote "A Visit From St. Nicholas" in 1822.

The new DiMenna Children's History Center, slated to open November 2011, is based on the idea that kids are interested in other kids. Using kiosks, touch screens, objects, toys, photographs, videos, and more, children are introduced to major and not so major figures in history when they were young. Meet Alexander Hamilton when he was a student coming to NYC for college, and Esteban Bellan, a New Yorker from Cuba, the first Latin American to play major-league baseball, who then introduced the game to Cuba. Call ahead to see if it's open.

If you like this sight, you might like the Guggenheim (#45).

EATS FOR KIDS Zabar's (2245 Broadway, tel. 212/787–2000) is the Upper West Side's go-to shop for classic NYC stapes like bagels, lox, and herring. You can also get sandwiches, cheeses, or their legendary Russian coffee cake. Bring it to Riverside Park for a picnic overlooking the Hudson River or to eat while playing at Hippo Playground. **Sarabeth's** (123 Amsterdam Ave., tel. 212/496–6280) is a crowd-pleaser, especially for brunch, when you can sample French toast, red omelets, or delectable pumpkin muffins.

NEW YORK PUBLIC LIBRARY

If there were an award for Most Underused NYC Resource, this would win. With a plethora of family programs throughout the library's 87 branches; dozens of child-centric reading rooms; and visits by celebrities, authors, and celebrity-authors; a visit to the NYPL should be at the top of your list. And don't worry, you don't need a local library card to participate.

The Main Library—on 42nd and 5th, guarded by its two iconic lion statues—is huge by Midtown standards and stocked with a collection so big you'd have to extend your visit by a few years to read every book. Not only does it have a Children's Center, but it also contains a permanent Winnie-the-Pooh exhibit. For a first birthday present, Christopher Robin Milne (A.A. Milne's son) was given a small teddy bear. Soon he was given four more friends (Eeyore, Piglet, Kanga, and Tigger). His father decided to use them in a bedtime story, and the rest, as we say, is history. The library displays all of them here.

Other branches with custom-designed children's centers are well worth a visit (especially on inclement-weather days). Visit St. Agnes (Upper West Side), Mulberry Street (a former

MAKE THE MOST OF YOUR TIME Go to the Web site to search for weekly recurring events and special happenings. Check nearby locations and also those slightly farther afield, as a quick subway ride may be all that stands between you and something free to do every day.

chocolate factory and a great place to read Dr. Seuss's *And To Think I Saw It on Mulberry Street*), and the brand new Battery Park City Library.

There's a fun activity for children almost every day of the week. For the youngest children, toddlers, preschool and below, there are usually morning storytimes.

For school-age children, K–6, the offerings expand greatly to include arts and crafts, computer classes, movies, game sessions (including both traditional games, e.g., chess/board games, and modern video games), knitting, reading aloud, karaoke, gardening, and storytime.

Special events (called "Touring Programs") are limited in location and regularity, often repeating fewer than four times. Recent events have included Mario Batali reading to kids, a performance of Czech fairytales complete with marionettes, Mad Science workshops, book making, stamp making, and face painting.

If you like this sight, you may also like the Books of Wonder (#65).

KEEP IN MIND
Along with Starbucks and chain bookstores, most library branches have restrooms and make a good place duck into when you need to make a pit stop.

EATS FOR KIDS If you're visiting the main branch, **Zeytinz** (24 W. 40th St., tel. 212/575–8080) is a deli with the usual suspects of sandwiches, salads, and more to buy and eat at Bryant Park tables or on the lawn. After they finish their greens, head to **The Treat Truck,** a roving sugar operation featuring nostalgic sweets like jammies (cookies with filling) and brownies is usually at either 38th & 5th Ave. (Tu and Th) or 45th & 6th Ave. (W and F). Check www.treatstruck.com for the latest location.

NEW YORK TRANSIT MUSEUM

Ask any local kid what their favorite museum is and they'll likely skip over the big-name attractions—the Met, the MoMA—to mention this tiny spot.

Why? Well with cut-away buses, vintage subway cars, and all sorts of levers and steering wheels they can operate, it's more "playground" than "museum." Even kids who aren't obsessed with trains, buses, and other wheeled things will love coming here and jumping into "traffic."

Housed in a decommissioned 1936 Brooklyn subway station, this is an interactive experience giving kids a tactile understanding of the history of public transportation in New York City and beyond. Expect to see 100 years of transit history and memorabilia including 19 restored subway cars dating from 1904 to 1964, antique turnstiles, a working signal tower, and a surface transportation room.

There are weekly children's programs where guides lead children in an art, storytelling, film, or movement activity covering popular topics like tokens, bridges, subway tiles, trains, or maps.

EATS FOR KIDS An ode to British fish-and-chips fare, the **ChipShop** (129 Atlantic Ave., tel. 718/855-7775) has an entire menu for kids, including mac and cheese for the seafood-squeamish. For a real treat, grab a scoop of organic ice cream at **Blue Marble** (420 Atlantic Ave., tel. 718/858-1100)—the strawberry has real berries in it—and hit their kids' play area filled with toys.

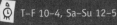
For a real thrill, and to make the past and present collide, conclude your visit with one of their community tours or nostalgia rides. Take a vintage train to a popular destination like Coney Island or the Rockaways. Tours (children 5 and up) pull the curtain back on the transit system and important transport places as seen through history by giving you an insider's view at things like the Westchester Yards (the 14,000-square-foot subway maintenance shop), Staten Island's oddities, and South Ferry as seen through the eyes of the author of *Manhattan: A Natural History of New York City*.

If you like this sight, you may also like the *Intrepid* Sea, Air & Space Museum (#43).

MAKE THE MOST OF YOUR TIME

Go at off-peak times (Tuesdays, or early afternoons, when there are no school groups), or else your kids may get stuck waiting a while for their turn to be the "bus driver."

KEEP IN MIND If you can't make it out to Brooklyn, the Annex in Grand Central is good for a quick, free visit providing a glimpse at New York City's transportation life. There's only one exhibit, but it usually enraptures kids. Recent ones have included a holiday mechanical train show and "The Subway in Film." The shop is what most people come for, with unique souvenirs like T-shirts displaying a favorite subway line, authentic subway artifacts (signs, tokens), and just about everything imprinted with the subway map (shower curtain anyone?).

NOGUCHI MUSEUM & SOCRATES SCULPTURE GARDEN

Part of what sets this museum apart—aside from being the only museum in New York City devoted exclusively to sculpture—is how the building mimics the pathos of its namesake sculptor, whose comprehensive collection is housed here.

Noguchi struggled to re-create the natural world in his work, and the building itself echoes that. Given that the garden is practically indistinguishable from the sculptures within it, he'd be proud.

Kids will enjoy this museum partially because Noguchi's pieces are so deeply tactile. The rough, broken edges of a carved pilar inside a smooth marble basin are enjoyable at any level. These graphic shapes don't require wall-text to understand.

KEEP IN MIND The museum's workshops are simply awesome, some of the best in the city. Get onto their e-mail list to be notified when registration opens and respond immediately; they sell out in literally hours.

MAKE THE MOST OF YOUR TIME The museum is petite, easily done in 30 minutes. To make the most of the contemplative nature of the space, have children bring pencils and sketchpads and inspire them to use the sculptures to channel their inner-artist.

32–37 Vernon Blvd., Queens

 Museum: 718/204-7088; www. noguchi.org. Garden: 718/956-1819; www.socratessculpturepark.org

 Museum: $10 adults, $5 seniors and students, free children under 12; Garden: free

 W–F 10–5, Sa–Su 11–6, Pay What You Wish first Friday of each month (June–Sept) 5:30–8; Garden 10–sunset, everyday

 2 and up

Another highlight of this museum for kids is unquestionably its art programs. These tend to book up far in advance. If possible, subscribe to their e-mail newsletter and sign up as soon as registration opens.

Visit the Socrates Sculpture Park a few blocks away to extend your art experience—it's one of the few places where kids are encouraged to touch the modern sculptures. In addition to this, it also offer a wide park space with a dazzling view of Manhattan. Check out a workshop to watch actual sculptors doing their thing.

If you like this sight, you may also like the Guggenheim (#45).

EATS FOR KIDS In summer parents can rejoice at the **Bohemian Hall & Beer Garden** (29–19 24th Ave., tel. 718/274-4925), where kids run amok as you chill with a draft beer in a giant outdoor courtyard with other local families. Or visit **Taverna Kyclades** (33-07 Ditmars Blvd., tel. 718/545-8666) for a wide variety of Greek specialties like stuffed grape leaves, kebabs, and pan-fried cheese.

PROSPECT PARK

Central Park gets all the fame, but this park, which shares the same designers (Olmsted and Vaux), is Brooklyn's pride and joy. Its 585 acres are equally satisfying for a 10-minute dash or a day-long excursion.

Visiting families should hit these highlights:

The 1912 carousel (Apr–Oct) has 51 horses, a lion, a giraffe, and a deer, as well as two dragon-drawn chariots, all brought to life by master carver Charles Carmel.

The Prospect Park Audubon Center lets kids dive into nature with sculptural birds and squirrels for kids to pose in. It's also home to great programming for kids, including bird-watching, nature crafts, and, in summer, periodic Twilight Tours, where kids can spot bats and other nocturnal creatures. This is also where you pick up the Electric Boat Tours of Brooklyn's only freshwater lake ($4 13 and up, $2 4–12; May–Oct).

Every Sunday (2 PM–dusk) conga drummers continue a tradition started in 1968. Musicians and dancers gather for a weekly drumming circle in Drummer's Grove (near the Parkside

MAKE THE MOST OF YOUR TIME Prospect Park's attractions are very spread out, not concentrated in one area like Central Park's. Either pick one or two attractions to do in an hour or so, or plan on spending at least half a day here. Also note that there are no pedicabs here; you'll be walking most of the way yourself!

Eastern Pkwy. and Grand Army Plaza, Brooklyn

 718/965–8999 hotline, 718/965–8969
for permit information, 718/287–3400
Audubon Center; www.prospectpark.org

 Free; some
attractions charge

Daily sunrise–1 AM

 All ages

Ave. subway stop) and kids are encouraged to join in dancing or drumming. (People will kindly loan their drums.)

Kensington Stables offers lessons and pony rides every day from 10 AM to sunset. Advance reservations are recommended, but you might get lucky as a walk-up ($3 for a pony ride; $47 per hour group lesson; semi-private $52; private lessons $57 or $34 per half hour).

Lefferts House (built in the 1800s by a Dutch family) takes kids back in time 200 years with traditional toys, tools, and games.

Wollman Rink—Brooklyn's only outdoor rink—is open for ice skating mid-November through March. The rest of the year families can rent pedal boats for touring the lake.

If you like this sight, you may also like Central Park (#57).

KEEP IN MIND
Visiting families with more time might want to tack on a trip to Prospect Park Zoo (#18) or nearby Brooklyn Botanic Garden (#62) or Brooklyn Museum (#59).

EATS FOR KIDS To the west of Prospect Park is Park Slope, otherwise known as StrollerLand to New Yorkers. This area is dominated by young families, which means restaurants here welcome little diners and cater to their tastes. Fifth Avenue is the "hood's" main drag, and you'll be spoiled for choice. Reliable regulars include Italian classics at **Al Di La Trattoria** (248 5th Ave., tel. 718/638–8888) or the **ChipShop** (129 Atlantic Ave., tel. 718/855–7775) for British fish-and-chips.

PROSPECT PARK ZOO

The Wildlife Conservation Society (parent organization to the zoos in Central Park, Queens, Prospect Park, and Bronx, and New York Aquarium) keeps its zoos distinct by distributing different animals in each property. Naturally, the biggest mammals are mostly restricted to the Bronx Zoo and aquatic animals to the Aquarium. The smaller animals, or animals requiring less living space, can be found scattered in the five boroughs. (With the exception of sea lions, which seem to be everywhere!)

Go to the Prospect Park Zoo (12 acres of naturalistic habitats) to see kangaroos and wallabies you won't see elsewhere. Both the Australian kangaroos and rock wallabies are found on Discovery Trail. Activities for kids to do here include burrowing in Plexiglas-topped tunnels, popping up next to a prairie dog, or leap-frogging across giant lily pads to goose nests. In the 2,500-foot aviary at trail's end, look for free-flying African birds and peacocks.

KEEP IN MIND It's always wise to wipe young hands frequently during visits here. Carry nonalcohol wet wipes or dampened washcloths in zip-lock bags for quick hand swiping before snack time or lunch.

MAKE THE MOST OF YOUR TIME The location of this zoo is ideal for a day out with the kids. Within a few minutes' walk are the Brooklyn Museum, Brooklyn Library, Children's Museum, and Brooklyn Botanical Garden. Not to mention the carousel and other kid-friendly fun Prospect Park has on offer.

 450 Flatbush Ave.,
Prospect Park, Brooklyn

 718/399-7339;
www.prospectparkzoo.org

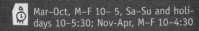 $8 ages 13 and up, $5
children 3–12, children
under 3 free, $6 seniors

Mar–Oct, M–F 10– 5, Sa–Su and holidays 10–5:30; Nov-Apr, M–F 10–4:30

 All ages

The Animal Lifestyles building is home to air, water, and land animals, including reptiles,
amphibians, fish, birds, and small mammals. The standout is the 4,500-square-foot hamadryads
baboon exhibit. You're only a thin sheet of glass away from these primates. Don't be surprised
if a friendly baboon approaches the glass to study you back.

In the barnyard the young crowd can peek into the chicken coop or meet goats, sheep,
and cows. A must-see are the California sea lions frolicking in a rocky California coast–
like environment. They are fed daily at 11:30, 2, and 4.

If you like this sight, you may also like the Queens Zoo (#15).

EATS FOR KIDS When the line is bearable (midweek) and the
kids aren't starving, walk the three blocks to **Tom's Diner** (782 Washington
Ave., tel. 718/636–9738), no relation to Suzanne Vega. Load up on carbs and
calories with fluffy pancakes, milk shakes, and other diner food done right.

PUPPETWORKS

For more than 35 years the Puppetworks, Inc., under the artistic direction of Nicolas Coppola, has been known throughout the country for it's mostly marionette productions. In 1987 Puppetworks opened a permanent 75-seat theater in a Park Slope (Brooklyn) storefront, next to the Puppetworks workshop. This informal and family-friendly theater presents daily performances of children's literature classics, with weekdays reserved for groups (20 or more).

Classic puppet theater favorites like *Puss in Boots* and *Pinocchio* round-out a year-long program that might also include *The Wizard of Oz, The Frog Prince, Peter and the Wolf,* and *The Emperor's Nightingale.* Each production is faithful to its source, whether that's fairy tales, children's literature, or folk tales.

Just two puppeteers are responsible for each performance, and while each show averages 13 puppet characters, some have had up to 68 puppets. Professionally designed sets with

EATS FOR KIDS For comfort food and diner delights (fluffy Belgian waffles, bacon-wrapped meat loaf, and stick-to-your ribs BBQ ribs), visit **Dizzy's** (511 9th St., tel. 718/499–1966). **Tomato and Basil** (226 4th Ave., tel. 718/596–8855) is perfect for pizza, and **Miriam** (79 5th Ave., tel. 718/622–2250) is delicious for Israeli cuisine or eggs and omelets anytime.

distinctive painted backdrops and intricate puppet costumes give the feeling of a scaled-down Broadway show. At the end of many performances a professional puppeteer will bring out one of the beautiful, hand-carved puppets to show to the audience, giving a brief behind-the-scenes—or, more accurately, above-the-strings—talk about the workings of a puppet theater. Children are encouraged to ask questions. The walls of the theater also display close to 100 marionettes used in past performances, though many are reused and recostumed.

If you like this sight, you may also like the New Victory Theater (#29).

MAKE THE MOST OF YOUR TIME

Age recommendations for each performance are listed on the Web site, along with a schedule of shows, dates, and times. The performances here are interactive, with nothing scary, so no need to worry about nightmares.

KEEP IN MIND Since 1976, when Macy's built a gingerbread puppet theater for Puppetworks, more than 50,000 children and their families have attended the annual Puppetworks Christmas performances. Bring your family to the ninth floor of Macy's Herald Square (Broadway at 34th St., tel. 212/695–4400) and start a new tradition. The holiday-theme performances are given 10 times daily and cost only a few dollars.

QUEENS MUSEUM

16

Families heading to the New York Hall of Science or Alley Pond Environmental Center absolutely must pass through here. While the majority of the museum is fine, the real draw is a miraculous miniature city—The Panorama.

Imagine giving your kids unlimited Legos, a 10,000-square-foot table, turning on Google maps (street view), then throwing in a little electricity, and you'll begin to picture what's on display here. It's the most magnificent replica of New York City you will see anywhere.

On a massive platform, the Panorama is an architectural model of the five boroughs of the city, and every single building (before 1992) is represented. Yes, every single one from the grand (Empire State) to the teeny average three-floor town house is on there, totaling 895,000 individual structures.

Most of the other civic and natural city features are there as well, including bridges, parks, rivers, roads, tugboats, stadiums, and more. It was commissioned by Robert Moses for the

MAKE THE MOST OF YOUR TIME

The first Sunday of every month is MetLife First Sundays for Families. Recent activities have included meeting the collaborative team behind the Curse of Bigness exhibit and seeing a Toy Theater in action.

EATS FOR KIDS Empanada Cafe (56–27 Van Doren St., tel. 718/592–7288) is known as the "United Nations of Empanadas," with over 20 varieties including organic and vegetarian options. The prices can't be beat (most are under $2).

73–50 Little Neck Pkwy., Floral Park

 Free; some events charge

 M–F 10–5 outdoors only, Sa–Su 10–5 house tours

 718/347-FARM; www.queensfarm.org

1 and up

1964 World's Fair with a contract stipulating there be no more than one percent margin of error between reality and model—talk about pressure! One hundred people working for Lester Associates built it originally, and the same company then updated it in 1992, changing 60,000 structures. The coolest change was made in 2006, allowing it to be displayed in different light conditions to highlight different buildings or areas and to re-create sounds of the city. And you may spot planes taking off and landing at the airport, as they travel along a transparent string.

On weekends the museum runs family drop-in art workshops (not connected to the Panorama).

If you like this sight, you may like Historic Richmond Town (#44).

KEEP IN MIND The best bargain in Manhattan real estate is in Queens. For $50 you can "own" any apartment you like on the Panorama. You will get a deed to the "property" (which makes a cute souvenir) and be acknowledged for at least five years. Bigger donations allow you to own icons like the Brooklyn Bridge. All funds go toward the maintenance, modernization, and upkeep of the Panorama.

QUEENS ZOO

Just as the Bronx Zoo's majesty lies in its largeness, this zoo's charm comes from intimacy—making it easily doable in under two hours. The compact layout, dearth of crowds, integrated climbing and play structures, impeccably clean petting zoo, and (in summer) proximity to a carousel, paddle-boat lake, and fountain, make it a favorite for time-constrained families or those with small children.

There's only one circular path to follow, so it's almost impossible to get lost. Two big benefits are the closeness to the animals (while still giving them relatively large living spaces) and the well-picked, unusual selection of animals kids won't normally see up close (including owls, two bald eagles, and a mountain lion). Along the path there are plenty of structures specifically designed for children's play, including a balance beam, climbing pyramid, and "Conservation Stations," where kids learn tips on saving the earth through interactive questions and games.

A definite favorite here is the impeccably clean and spacious farm animals section (petting zoo). Come in spring and you just might see some newborn lambs.

MAKE THE MOST OF YOUR TIME The zoo is next to the New York Hall of Science (#24), both in Flushing Meadows–Corona Park. Combine your visit to either place with a stop at the nearby Queens Museum (#16) to see the 10,000-square-foot miniature model of New York City—complete with 895,000 tiny buildings and landmarks.

53-51 111th St., Flushing Meadows–Corona Park, Flushing, Queens

 718/271-1500; www.queenszoo.com

 $8 adults, $5 children 3–12, $6 seniors

 Mar 27–Oct 31, M–F 10–5, Sa, Su, and holidays 10–5:30; Nov–Mar 26, 10–4:30 daily

 All ages

Highlights of a visit here include:

Great Plains: With giant bison, a coyote, and a pronghorn antelope that can run 55 MPH, this captures "home on the range."

Aviary: This geodesic dome designed by Buckminster Fuller for the 1964 World's Fair, is now home to ducks, turkeys, porcupines, cardinals, and egrets.

South American Trail: The adorable pudu particularly likes visitors, and will often come right up to the glass to interact with kids. See if kids can spot the bear hiding in the trees.

Sea lion feedings: These happen every day at 11:15 AM, 2 PM, and 4 PM. On weekends the Discovery Center, filled with books, games, a microscope, fossils, and a craft station, is open noon–4 PM.

If you like this sight, you may also like the Staten Island Zoo (#8).

KEEP IN MIND
Among the other zoo animals in the Great Plains section is Otis, a coyote rescued from Central Park in 1999. He now safely resides here, away from cross-town yellow cabs.

EATS FOR KIDS Feed your animal appetite at the cafeteria, overlooking the sea-lion pool. Grab a vanilla and hot fudge shake at **Joe's Best Burger** (39–11 Main St., tel. 718/445–8665) or try the **Omonia Café** (32–20 Broadway, Astoria, tel. 718/274–6650) for a light bite of Greek food. The cake for the movie *My Big Fat Greek Wedding* was created here.

RADIO CITY MUSIC HALL

To get behind the scenes of this lavish art deco palace that's home to the high-kicking Rockettes you'll want to take the Stage Door Tour. Along the way you'll learn about this landmark, the brainchild of theatrical impresario S. L. "Roxy" Rothafel. Radio City was the first building in the Rockefeller Center complex, and it was the world's largest indoor theater in 1932. In 1999 it was renovated to the tune of $70 million. Tours showcase the building's technological capabilities as well as its history. Luminaries such as Frank Sinatra, Ella Fitzgerald, and Sammy Davis Jr. have graced this stage, as have contemporary artists like Sheryl Crow.

To whet your appetite, here are some amazing Radio City facts: the shimmering gold curtain is the largest theatrical curtain on earth. The mighty Wurlitzer organ, built in 1932, has two consoles, each weighing 2½ tons. Its pipes, some of which are 32 feet tall, are housed in 11 rooms. Look up and you can see a 24-carat gold-leaf ceiling glistening 60 feet

MAKE THE MOST OF YOUR TIME

Visiting Radio City Music Hall during the winter months is magical. Combine your trip with walking around or ice-skating at Rockefeller Center, visiting the holiday windows along 5th Avenue, or browsing at F.A.O. Schwarz.

EATS FOR KIDS With the plethora of office workers around here, it's an ideal place to do as the locals do—get lunch from one of the food trucks! Several trucks and carts around 53rd Street and 6th Avenue serve anything from authentic German sausage to whoopee pies. **Moshe's Falafel** (46th St. and 6th Ave.) has been ranked one of the best by the local press, and with three falafels for under $4 it's a steal.

above you. For the record, the Music Hall contains over 25,000 light bulbs inside; outside, the marquee is a block long and uses more than 6 miles of red and blue neon.

The Stage Door Tour also includes a visit to the private apartment of founder Roxy Rothafel and a stop in the costume shop, which contains outfits worn during the Radio City Christmas Spectacular. Your tour group will also meet a member of the Radio City Rockettes, who will share some of the company's history. One-hour tours depart from the main lobby at the corner of 6th Avenue and 50th Street.

Even if you don't take the tour, consider catching a stage show here and see all that technological wizardry at work.

If you like this sight, you may also enjoy the NBC Studios Tour (#30).

KEEP IN MIND In 1979, to save the Music Hall from the wrecking ball, the program format was changed from films and stage shows to live concerts, television specials, and events. The *Radio City Christmas Spectacular, Blues Clues, Dora the Explorer,* and adult and kids' concerts play to sold-out crowds throughout the year. You must purchase a ticket for children 2 and older for performances here, but for some events, like *Barney,* youngsters 1 and older require a ticket, even if they plan to sit in your lap for most of the show.

The price is outrageous, and the wait ranges from unpleasant to awful (depending on weather), but once you actually get to ice-skate under the golden statue of Prometheus while that gorgeous 80-plus-foot tree twinkles in the background, it's nothing short of breathtaking.

And when you think of how your kid will be able to say "I skated there!" every time he or she sees a movie set in New York City during the winter holidays, it becomes worth it to join the rite of passage that other family consider their holiday tradition.

Truth be told, it's really not all that bad, especially if you go during the lower traffic times (early mornings and weekdays before 5 PM or so). Going before the holiday season (from October until the end of November) is not only much less crowded, it's cheaper, with lower rates and occasional bargains. In former seasons they have offered a deal where noontime skaters pay $5 (rentals extra).

EATS FOR KIDS Dine at the Rink Cafe and Bar, open in summer 11–11, or the **Rock Center Café** (tel. 212/332–7620) year-round. **Dean & DeLuca** (1 Rockefeller Plaza, tel. 212/664–1363) serves quick sandwiches and snacks.

Bordered by 47th and 52nd Sts. and 5th and 7th Aves.; ice rink, between 49th and 50th Sts. and 5th and 6th Aves.

 Skating $10–$14 ages 12 and up, $7.50–$8.50 children 11 and under; skate rental $7.50

M–F 9 AM–12 AM, Sa–Su 8:30 AM–12 AM; call for session times

 212/332–7654 rink, 212/332–7655 lessons, 212/664–7174 tours

2 and up

Sessions are 1½ hours on a first-come, first-served basis. Skate and locker rentals, season passes, and multi-ticket books, lessons, and group rates are all available, as are birthday parties with skate admissions, rental, and refreshments (January–April). During summer the rink turns into the Rink Bar, serving cocktails and bar bites. Children are admitted, but the atmosphere is far more for adults.

The ice rink is just a small part of Rockefeller Center. Top of the Rock is often considered a better alternative to the Empire State Building, with a great view, timed tickets, and no lines. Other things to explore here include NBC Studios Tour (#30) and dozens of shops and restaurants, including the Nintendo World Lego stores.

If you like this sight, you may also like Central Park (#57).

KEEP IN MIND
Other great spots for a twirl on the ice are the Lasker and Wollman Memorial rinks (see Central Park, #57); Sky Rink; and Brooklyn's Wollman Rink (see Prospect Park, #19), not to be confused with the Wollman Memorial Rink in Central Park.

MAKE THE MOST OF YOUR TIME Monday through
Thursday, lunchtime skating is a bargain at $5. Not as much of a bargain, but worth the price, is the Top of the Rock (30 Rockefeller Plaza, tel. 212/698–2000); its six-level observatory has floor-to-ceiling windows permitting breathtaking views of city landmarks. Tickets are $17.50 for adults and $11.25 for children 6–12.

RUBIN MUSEUM

Telling kids you're going to see Himalayan art is the world's biggest buzzkill. Even families sporting "Free Tibet" stickers on their VW's don't get excited about the idea of shuffling through exhibitions with titles like "The Nepalese Legacy in Tibetan Painting."

But don't let a little lofty language stop you from the enchanting tales your kids can discover, like the one about the Tiger Rider who gave up his kingdom to be with an outcast woman, only to be asked to return and rule again. Or the Dog Lover who left a luxurious paradise to live in a cave with his beloved canine companion, only to have her turn into a beautiful woman . . .

The museum exposes kids to Himalayan culture through the area's heritage of oral and visual storytelling, and that makes their family-friendly events even more compelling. Once weekly (currently on Wednesdays) children (4–6 years) travel to the Himalayas through their imagination during "Word Play" when a master storyteller leads the group. Younger

KEEP IN MIND A few times a year the museum holds Family Days, with a slew of family-friendly activities. And on October 2, the anniversary of the museum's founding, they hold a day-long art and peacemaking "extravaganza" known as the International Day of Non-Violence.

MAKE THE MOST OF YOUR TIME Set aside some time to walk through Union Square, only a few blocks away. In summer this popular park gets crowded, but with reason; it contains a fun, brand-new playground, a massive farmers' market (Mondays, Wednesdays, Fridays, and Saturdays), and a popular dog run, always ringed with cooing animal-lovers. In winter, around the holidays, there is a terrific outdoor market filled with handmade items.

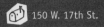 150 W. 17th St.

 $10 adult, $7 seniors and artists, $2 students June–Sept, free F 6–10 and free to seniors first M of each month

 M and Th 11–5, W 11–7, F 11–10, Sa and Su 11–6

212/620–5000; www.rmanyc.org

All ages

children (2–4) look and touch objects inspired by the museum's collection in Yak Packers. Toddlers (3–4) use movement to express their thoughts about visual art in Movement Through Art Early Childhood program. On weekends kids 6 and up create a painting, collage, or other works of art after getting inspiration from the galleries.

The galleries can be done in 20–45 minutes, perfect for little ones' attention spans.

Pick up enchanting, affordable items like Buddha water-painting kits and bead bracelets in the gift shop.

If you like this sight, you may also like Karma Kids Yoga (#41).

EATS FOR KIDS Save your appetite for the outstanding fare at **City Bakery** (3 W. 18th St., tel. 212/366–1414). After an obligatory-but-delicious lunch of vegetables, salads, sandwiches, or other salad-bar staples, it's time to reward yourself with a face-sized chocolate-chip cookie, thick-as-mud hot chocolate, or their signature pretzel croissants—a France-meets-the-Fatherland treat that's flaky, dense, sweet, buttery, and salty all at once.

SNUG HARBOR

Everyone loves to take the Staten Island Ferry, but 99.9% of its tourist passengers just turn around and get right back on and return to Manhattan.

Then Staten Island got smart. A few years back someone decided that visitors would venture here more often if the main attractions were easier to reach. This 83-acre former retirement center for seamen was restored, and now it's home to many kid-friendly institutions.

Start at the Staten Island Children's Museum. Ideal for those under 7, it's a good balance between indoor playground, nature exploration, and hands-on. Favorite areas include the Block Harbor (play on a pirate ship), Bugs & Other Insects (see bees working or move into an ant apartment), and a real stage (put on costumes and perform). During warmer months the Sea of Boats outdoor playground is a small water-play area. Most days they have one or two interactive programs for kids to participate in. Often animals from the Staten Island Zoo will come visit, or kids will be called on to do a science, cooking, or art project.

EATS FOR KIDS Get a table with a water view at **R.H. Tugs** (1115 Richmond Terr., tel. 718/447–6369). Across the street from Snug Harbor, it has the best views of New York City's working harbor (yes, including many tugboats, barges, boats, and more) your kids will ever see. The food is fine, but secondary, as your boat-fascinated kids will be engrossed in the real action happening on the water.

Snug Harbor Cultural Center,
1000 Richmond Terr., Staten Island

 Varies by attraction

 Varies by attraction

718/448-2500;
www.snug-harbor.org

 1 and up

The Noble Maritime Museum is a lesser-known attraction that has recently been renovated with a strong eye toward visiting families. Named for John A. Noble, an artist and lover of everything maritime, this spot allows kids to adopt a sailor's persona for a few hours. Don't miss the tugboat cabin (where kids get to be captain), Noble's houseboat studio (a look at life on a teeny vessel), the Crosswalk Gallery (objects have been intentionally placed lower and wall text is written with a younger audience in mind), and the numerous ship models.

On warmer days, visit the Botanical Gardens. Start at the Chinese Scholar's Garden with its dramatic black pagoda and pond, then wander the grounds. It's compact, and can be done easily in an hour.

If you like this sight, you might also like the Children's Museum of Manhattan (#54).

MAKE THE MOST OF YOUR TIME

Take the S40 bus for about 2 miles to the Snug Harbor stop. Or on really nice days, with older kids accustomed to walking, you can walk that distance. It's a nice scenic trip along New York Harbor.

KEEP IN MIND The Staten Island Museum is reputed to be moving here, but no one is willing to set a date for that event. Until then, if you have time before the ferry, stop in on your way to Snug Harbor or back to the ferry landing. (It's across the street from the terminal). More eccentric-old-mad-scientist's-collection than museum, this is really a grouping of curiosities. There are some paintings and plenty of local interest items, but what kids will beg to see is the room of fluorescent rocks that glow when the room goes dark.

SONY WONDER TECHNOLOGY LAB

10

From the moment you step into the lobby atrium of Sony Wonder Technology Lab, you feel the excitement of cutting-edge communication technology.

First kids make a personal profile that follows them throughout the lab. Then—à la Disney circa 1975—using extensive lighting, color, and sound effects, the exhibit leads kids down a "path" of data (e.g., e-mail, music, downloads) throughout cyberspace.

Experiences kids can try as they travel the lab include singing, making music with electronic instruments, designing video games, making movies, and playing with the latest PlayStation games.

Of most interest to older kids and adults are the interactive exhibits such as Robot Zone (programming robots), Animation Studio (make a short animation), Virtual Surgery (just like it sounds), and the two favorites of all ages: Dance Motion Capture (you dance, a Sony animated character mimics your movements) and WSWL Production Studio (be a part of a television newscast).

EATS FOR KIDS In Sony Plaza, **Starbucks** offers sandwiches and pastries. If you can brave the often long lines, visit **Serendipity 3** (225 E. 60th St., tel. 212/838–3531) for dessert, ice-cream treats, and their famous frozen hot chocolate.

MAKE THE MOST OF YOUR TIME Tickets are required for admission and are often booked far in advance. Try to book when reservations first open, 3 months before your desired visit, by calling 212/833–8100 Tuesday–Friday, 9 AM–2 PM. A minimum number of same-day tickets are available from the walk-up window beginning 10 AM Tuesday–Saturday and noon on Sunday.

 550 Madison Ave.

 Free

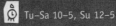 Tu–Sa 10–5, Su 12–5

 212/833-8100;
www.sonywondertechlab.com

All ages

On Saturdays and select other days there are two feature film screenings, one for mature audiences and one for very young children (e.g., *Sesame Street*).

The Tech in the Plaza workshops are some of the most extraordinary technology programs around. Children 8 and up get to dismantle a piece of electronic equipment to see what's inside and how it works. Although free and registration isn't required, space is limited, so get there early. Other workshops include building robots for ages 9 and up and crafts for the youngest kids.

The enormous SONY building lobby also happens to be a favorite gathering place to let toddlers run free during cold weather.

If you like this sight, you may also like F.A.O. Schwarz (#48).

KEEP IN MIND Sony's good-hearted attempt to woo children away from an almost certain future Apple addiction (not that they'll admit it) will be seen as either hokey or happening, depending on your child's age and electronic sophistication. Parents with kids over 10 should check out the Web site before deciding on a visit.

SOUTH STREET SEAPORT MUSEUM

9

It's hard to remember that NYC is a port city, what with all the yellow cabs and bike messengers zooming about on land. But visiting the South Street Seaport Museum's three historic vessels in the harbor (the *Peking,* a large sailing cargo ship; the *Ambrose;* and the *W.O. Decker,* a 1930 tugboat) is a very real reminder for kids. Doing activities on these vessels lets kids see how sailors and the maritime industry worked in previous centuries.

In summer, children (9 and up) love to do one of the "Programs Afloat": The two-hour interactive sails on the *Pioneer* schooner have everyone pitching in to man the boat and kids learn about the history of the harbor and environmental responsibility. On the one-hour tour kids discover the hidden corners of New York's working waterfront aboard the tugboat *W.O. Decker* (a real NY tugboat built in Queens). Or for older teens and adults, the extended four-hour trip on the tugboat explores what feels like every crevice of the NY area waterways, including industrial archaeological and wildlife sights.

EATS FOR KIDS Go local by walking a block up to Front and Beekman streets. Several original, non-chain restaurants that cover the four kid food groups like pizza at **Il Brigante** (214 Front St., 212/285–0222), sandwiches at **Stella Maris** (213 Front St., 212/233–2417), pub food at **Jeremy's Ale House** (228 Front St., 212/964–3537), and chicken fingers at **Cowgirl Seahorse** (259 Front St., 212/608–7873).

Pier 16 Visitors' Center, 12 Fulton St.

 212/748-8600;
www.southstseaportmuseum.org

 $12 ages 13 and up,
$8 children 5–12,
$10 students and seniors,
free under 5

 Jan–Mar F–M 10–5, 12–4 to
board the historic ships;
Apr–Dec T–Su 10–6

3 and up

The exhibit space rotates shows focusing on ships, like memorabilia of the cruise liner *Normandie* or the ship collection of F.D.R. It's interesting but not worth the museum's entrance fee alone.

Other programs run by the museum for children include a toddler playgroup, workshops teaching basic sailors' skills (navigation, weather conditions), crafts programs, and peeks into the environmental world of the East River.

Alas, this area's subway station ("Fulton Street") is the only remnant of the East Coast's largest and most important wholesale fish market, Fulton Fish Market, 1822–1950s. However, the romance of the sea is still very alive here as long as you dodge the generic commercialism.

If you like this sight, you might also like the New York Aquarium (#28).

MAKE THE MOST OF YOUR TIME

Visit their Web site in advance to pick the day and time of your visit. Many of the most enjoyable activities require reservations and book up quickly.

KEEP IN MIND For children under 10, one of the most compelling reasons to visit the area is more about air than water. Little Airplane Productions (207 Front St., tel. 212/965–8999)—the producers of shows including *The Wonder Pets!*—opens its studios on Tuesdays and Thursdays (and occasional Saturdays) to kids for an interactive tour of their creative process. Inside a gorgeously restored original brownstone kids learn step-by-step how a preschool show is created and get to do hands-on activities including drawing, designing, animating, and being the voice-over for an in-process design.

STATEN ISLAND ZOO

Of all the city's zoos, this is the only one that has retained its Old World feel—for better or worse—with the aura of an old European zoo. And the good part is it feels intimate and low key. You can sit for hours without any crowds; there are no lines; the buildings are low-slung, covered in ivy; and the landscaping makes winding paths. Perhaps the biggest indicator of old-worldliness: the gift shop is so well hidden, and so teeny, you practically have to beg to find it.

The down side? Some of the animals are definitely in enclosures far too small for them. Theoretically, the zoo is working to move them to happier pastures, but for now it can be a bonus for kids who want to feel close enough to touch the whiskers of a big cat.

The Kids' Korral and Children's Center are petting areas with the usual farm animals, like goats, llamas, and chickens. A quick pony ride is next door as well.

MAKE THE MOST OF YOUR TIME

Plan your day at the zoo so you don't miss the action during feeding times. Check the feeding time schedules listed at the entry gates.

EATS FOR KIDS The 48 bus stop is a few feet from **Metro Pizza** (1218 Forest Ave., tel. 718/720–3010), where they toss up some of healthiest and tastiest pizza on Staten Island. But more importantly, it's next door to **The Cookie Jar** (1226 Forest Ave., tel. 718/448–3500), a cubbyhole lined with 200+ cookie jars that would make any collector drool. The cases are filled with 150+ varieties of cookies, bars, and cupcakes, giving your kids something too drool over, too.

614 Broadway, Staten Island

 $8 ages 15–59, $5 children 3–14, $6 seniors, free under 3, free W after 2, parking free

Daily 10–4:45

718/442–3100;
www.statenislandzoo.org

 All ages

Find things that slink and slither at the Carl Kaufeld Serpentarium, with its internationally acclaimed display of reptiles, including one of the most extensive collections of North American rattlesnakes anywhere.

The African Savannah exhibit re-creates this ecosystem at twilight and features meerkats, a burrowing python, leopards, bush babies, and rock hyrax—curious creatures that look like rodents but are actually related to elephants. The Tropical Forest exhibit highlights the endangered South American rain forest and its resident animals. Watch the piranha, spider monkeys, short-tailed leaf-nosed fruit bats, and iguanas in a natural flow of flora and fauna. At the Otter Exhibit, North American river otters perform their antics from above and below the underwater viewing tank.

If you like this sight, you may also like the Queens Zoo (#15).

KEEP IN MIND Clove Lake Park is across the street, and includes a playground, a lake with boat rides, and even an ice-skating rink. Combine this with your zoo trip, ferry ride, and the Cookie Jar—snack stop, and you have the perfect Staten Island day.

STATUE OF LIBERTY

"Give me your tired, your poor, / Your huddled masses yearning to breathe free. . . ." Many people recognize the opening lines of the 1883 Emma Lazarus poem "The New Colossus," which is inscribed on a plaque inside the Statue of Liberty Museum. And everyone recognizes the sentiment. For more than 100 years this historic monument has served as a universal beacon of hope and opportunity, a symbol of freedom, and a gift of international friendship.

Kids 8 and up may enjoy a ranger-guided tour. The promenade tour includes the museum in the pedestal's lobby, where the statue's original torch resides, as well as a visit to the promenade, which has great views of the statue and New York Harbor. The observatory tour covers much of the promenade tour plus an elevator ride to the pedestal observatory, with more awesome views, and a lighted view up into the copper interior of the statue. Kids 7–12 who could be impatient in a lengthy group presentation may be happier taking their own self-guided tour as Junior Rangers; a free booklet, available at the Liberty Island Information Center walks kids through the tour.

MAKE THE MOST OF YOUR TIME Getting tickets far in advance is easy, fast, and a must. Visit www.statuecruises.com to see available dates and times, and add options like the audio tour or a visit to Ellis Island.

Liberty Island, New York Harbor

 Tickets and monument passes (tel. 877–LADY TIX; www.statuecruises.com); Statue of Liberty information (tel. 212/363–3200; www.nps.gov)

 Free; ferry fees $12 ages 13 and up, $5 children 4–12; time passes required to enter the Statue of Liberty

 Daily 9–5

 4 and up

One of the main reasons to visit the statue, of course, is to view this monument to freedom up close. A museum here features exhibits detailing how the statue was built, and the promenade, colonnade, and top level of the pedestal offer spectacular views of New York Harbor. Life-size castings of the face and foot of the statue are available for sight-impaired visitors to feel. A "timed pass" reservation system is run by the National Park Service for visitors who want to enter the monument. Timed passes are not required to visit the grounds. A limited number of timed passes are available from the ferry company daily on a first-come, first-serve basis. Or you can get a timed-pass reservation online by visiting *www.statuecruises. com*. As she always has, Lady Liberty welcomes all.

If you like this sight, you may also like Ellis Island (#50).

KEEP IN MIND
Most children under 12 will not have the stamina to do both Liberty and Ellis Island.

EATS FOR KIDS Have a big meal before you go, and bring snacks so the kids will be able to hold out until you return to the mainland. Once back, head to Stone Street, a pedestrian-only cobblestone lane lined with great restaurants. There's pizza at **Adrienne's Pizza Bar** (54 Stone St., tel. 212/248–3038), French café pastries and light lunch at **Financier** (62 Stone St., tel. 212/344–5600), pub food at **Stone Street Tavern** (52 Stone St., tel. 212/785–5658), and even Swedish at **Smorgas Chef** (53 Stone St., tel. 212/422–3500).

SYMPHONY SPACE

Take a good long look at New York City parents. For every pinstripe-suited mom or clean-cut dad there's at least one tattooed former rocker pushing a stroller. These are parents who cut their teenage teeth at spots like CBGBs, the Beacon, or the Fillmore. Now that their iPods have slightly more Baby Einstein and slightly less Johnny Rotten, they need a venue to indoctrinate their future Rolling Stone. And that's where Symphony Space comes in.

Symphony Space is an incredible misnomer, as this is the site of several kid-friendly rockin' shows. For families, it's anything but a staid classical music spot—although it does have plenty of that for adults. At its heart, it's an Upper West Side institution where kids can spend part of every weekend dancing in the aisles, singing, cheering, getting up on stage, and generally preparing for the mosh pit.

During the school year there's at least one family event per week. Kid-friendly bands kick out the jams here and get their little fans up and moving. Expect a good mix of evergreen

MAKE THE MOST OF YOUR TIME
On warm days pair your show with some time at Riverside Park, only one block away. Less crowded than Central Park, it's a low-key way to take time out. There are several great playgrounds, meandering paths, and of course waterfront views.

EATS FOR KIDS On this patch of Broadway it's hard to find a restaurant that isn't family-friendly. **City Diner** (2441 Broadway, tel. 212/877–2720) is popular for its pancakes and diner food. A bit of a walk, but worth it, is **Popover Café** (551 Amsterdam Ave., tel. 212/595–8555). A big basket of fresh popovers and a plate of lemon pancakes will quash any hunger-induced meltdowns.

2537 Broadway between 95th and 96th Sts.

  Varies by show

 Mostly weekends, varies by show

212/864-5400;
www.symphonyspace.org

2 and up

favorites like Laurie Berkner and Dan Zanes and lesser-known newcomers like Captain Bogg and Salty and The Milkshakes.

Check their schedule for upcoming festivals. Occasionally they will hold free-form events for the whole family, such as the recent Korean Traditional Performing Arts Association 5th Annual Family Program.

During the summer, when most families head out of town or do outdoor activities, the schedule slims down and focuses less on live performances. It's mostly a place that comes alive during the school year.

If you like this sight, you may also like the New Victory Theater (#29).

KEEP IN MIND The other wildly popular event that takes place here is the New York International Children's Film Festival. Tickets for showings of these engaging and creative animated films sell out almost the minute they go on sale, with some seats available same day. If you're going to be in town sometime between December and February, this is definitely worth attending. Get on their e-mail list for first notification.

TOYS"R"US

5

Every town has a Toys"R"Us, but the flagship location in Times Square, decked out with an indoor Ferris wheel, brings the average shopping experience to a fantasyland level.

Follow the wisdom of local parents and come "to do," not "to buy." Since it stocks only the most mainstream of toys—albeit a super wide and deep variety of each—you're not here to cull out the obscure local finds,

Instead, come ready to play. The indoor 60-foot-high Ferris wheel with popular character cars is the main attraction; it's a refreshing value at $4, and lasts at least 10 minutes. Upstairs there's a Thomas the Tank play table, where they'll while away many hours if the weather is inclement (best for kids under 6). Steer teens and tweens to the ground floor, with its Nintendo and other video game stations.

Along the way, marvel at the gigantic animatronic Tyrannosaurus, the giant Lego Statue of Liberty and Empire State Building (complete with attacking King Kong), and a two-story

MAKE THE MOST OF YOUR TIME Like the rest of Times Square, this can be overrun with families and children hopped up on candy from the neighboring Hershey and M&M stores. To make your visit more pleasant, try going earlier in the day, when kids are less likely to have visited the candy emporiums. The Ferris wheel line is also shorter during this time.

1514 Broadway, at 44th St.

 Free, $4 for the Ferris Wheel

 M–Th and Su 10–9, F 10–11, Sa 9–11

646/366–8800;
www1.toysrus.com/timessquare

 All ages

Barbie dollhouse. And snap a photo with the brand's mascot Geoffrey (use your own camera and there's no charge).

For a once-in-a-lifetime experience, see your child in lights on Broadway. The Marquee Moment will put your child's picture and a special message on the gigantic LED screen on Broadway ($30 includes one 5x7 photo).

If you like this sight, you may also like F.A.O. Schwarz (#48).

KEEP IN MIND
For an affordable souvenir, go to the first floor near the exit. There you can personalize Toys"R"Us–logoed items like sticker books, key chains, and mugs with your child's name.

EATS FOR KIDS Times Square is synonymous with Tourist Trap. For better value, 6th Avenue is filled with office-worker lunch spots ranging from modern delis (build your own salad, pasta, sandwich, or pizza) to more upscale sit-down venues. For a lovely outdoor setting, try the **Bryant Park Café** (476 5th Ave., tel. 212/944–8215), outside the main branch of the public library.

UNITED NATIONS

4

Kids may not "get" abstract concepts like nationalism and political boundaries, or lofty goals like international human rights. But they definitely get sending postcards to friends and family with stamps you can't buy anywhere else in the world. They get seeing people in enchanting national dress, like flowing gold saris from India and brightly colored dashiki of South Africa. And they definitely get listening to words being translated into tens of other languages instantly.

As you approach the headquarters, point out the 192 different flags representing 192 different nations arranged alphabetically (from Afghanistan to Zimbabwe). Then, explain to your kids how it may feel like they are still in New York, but they are actually entering a different country, international land belonging to those 191 nations complete with its own security forces and post office with its own postage. You might want to play *I Spy* at the massive stained-glass window in the lobby, a Chagall creation. Kids will find symbols of peace

KEEP IN MIND

Before you leave, step into the post office to send home a souvenir: a postcard with stamps you can't get anywhere else in the world.

MAKE THE MOST OF YOUR TIME Next to the East River, the UN Building is far from any subway station, and getting cabs is almost impossible. The M15 and M50 buses will drop you off and pick you up right there. (You can use your MetroCard on all city buses.)

and music in the design. And definitely show them Foucault's pendulum and teach them that it proves the earth rotates.

Families with children 5 and up should begin by taking the tour. In a relatively quick 45 minutes you'll see the General Assembly, where the member nations meet, and, subject to the construction schedule: the Security Council Chamber, Trustee Council Chamber, Economic and Social Council Chamber, Rose Garden, and public concourse. There may also be a stop to see the gifts member nations have donated over the years.

If you like this sight, you may also like Ellis Island (#50).

EATS FOR KIDS Skip the UN Delegates dining room. It may have views of the East River, but it also has a strict dress code (no jeans, or shorts; jackets for men). Not exactly a spot to spread out coloring books. Instead, head back toward 1st Avenue, where you'll find affordable restaurants for all tastes. For a treat, walk a few blocks to **Buttercup Bakeshop** (973 2nd Ave., tel. 212/350–4144) to sample the city's best Rice Crispy treats and 20+ varieties of cupcakes.

VICTORIAN GARDENS

In summer, Wollman Rink transforms into a wonderful amusement park. There are three reasons why this is the ideal amusement park for young children. First, being contained in a skating rink, it has only one way in or out, making it a bit harder to lose children. Second, it's not only Manhattan's only amusement park, it also happens to be in the heart of Manhattan, making it easy to add a dash of fairground fun without an all-day excursion. Third, there are virtually no lines. Even on the busiest day the wait is less than five minutes.

Victoria Gardens has 14 rides, and almost all are appropriate for children of all ages. Best of all, there are no height restrictions. (Some rides do require a chaperone if your kid is under 42".)

Rides, like Convoy, a train; Red Baron, open airplanes kids can steer up or down; Fun Slide, a 30-foot-high plastic slide; Mini Mouse, a petite rollercoaster; Jump Around, a dune buggy bouncing up and down; Samba Balloon, think teacups that lift off the ground; Family Swinger, sort of a carousel made of swings; Hydro Racer, a boat going around a track while a man

MAKE THE MOST OF YOUR TIME Yes, there are more crowds on the weekend, but there's also more entertainment, so it's worth braving the lines for more mature younger kids (6–8). Go as early as you can and plan on staying about three hours. After that, almost everything has been done twice. Get a handstamp for all-day reentry. In the heat of a mid-August afternoon this can feel like Dante's Third Circle, so think about the weather before you commit.

Wollman Rink, Central Park

 212/982-2229;
www.victoriangardensnyc.com

$18.50 unlimited-entry (unlimited rides) weekdays, $21.50 weekends; single admission (pay-per-ride) $6.50 weekdays, $7.50 weekends; children under 36 inches free

June-Sept, M–F 11–7, Sa 10–9, Su 10–8, hours vary check Web site for details

 3 and up

sprays the riders; and Happy Swing, a row of seats that goes up and then free falls down, are all mild enough for kids of any age to ride alone.

Children under 42" must ride with an adult on a few rides, including Aeromax ("airplanes" offering views of the park), Kite Flyer (free flight in a reclining position), and Rockin' Tug (a whirling and turning boat ride adults may want to skip).

On weekends there are at least four shows a day by well-practiced children's entertainers. Two favorites that return year after year are *Jenny's Big Hula Hoop Show* (remarkable feats with 20+ hula hoops at once) and *King Henry's Magic Show*. Recently the entertainment options have broadened to include clowns, Wild West tricks, card tricks, and a variety of magicians.

If you like this sight, you may also like Coney Island (#52).

KEEP IN MIND
A wristband for unlimited rides is generally a better deal for children. However, if your kids are over 6 or 7 and prone to doing rides alone, you'll get better value by taking the admission-only option for yourself.

EATS FOR KIDS Outside food isn't allowed inside, but there are several wholesome and delicious places around Central Park South. Stop at one of them before or after a trip here, and you'll save your kids from overpriced hot dogs and other junk food. **Whole Foods** (10 Columbus Circle, tel. 212/823-9600) has a popular eat-in area with fresh-made all-natural pizzas, ethnic food bars (Indian, Chinese, Mexican), and rotisserie meats with vegetable sides. **Mickey Mantle's** (42 Central Park South, tel. 212/688-7777) is great for baseball fans, with surprisingly good diner-type food and walls of authentic memorabilia.

WAVE HILL

The American Museum of Natural History (#67), the National Park System, and teddy bears all owe a giant debt of gratitude to Wave Hill.

Back in the day (read: before income taxes) NYC's upscale residents escaped the heat by going to their summer compounds on the Hudson River. Wave Hill, a few minutes from Manhattan, is not only one of the most impressive of these, it's also rumored to be the place where young Teddy Roosevelt developed his passion for nature and the roots of his future conservation efforts (his family rented the home from 1870 to 1871). Overlooking the Hudson River and Palisades, this public garden spans 23 acres and includes a greenhouse, rock garden, lawns, an aquatic garden, Wave Hill House, education center, café, shop, and plenty of benches, picnic spots, pergolas, lawn chairs, and other lounging features.

Today, families visiting on weekends will find it's one of the easiest ways for parents to have a truly tranquil moment while the kids are kept happily engaged. Every Saturday

MAKE THE MOST OF YOUR TIME

Before you settle your plans, pick out a day with a good weather forecast, and keep in mind that Wave Hill is closed most Mondays.

EATS FOR KIDS Eating beforehand or bringing a picnic is the best food option for children. There is a walled outdoor picnic area. The small café is the only on-site food outlet, and while its local organic ingredients are delectable, it's best for adults (unless your kids fantasize about cured Thai salmon on seven-grain bread with lemongrass crème fraîche).

24 W. 249th St. and
Independence Ave., Bronx

 718/549-3200; www.wavehill.org

 $8 adults, $2 children 6 and up,
$4 students and seniors, free
select Target Tuesday and Saturday
mornings check Web site, $8
on-site parking, free shuttle

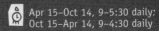 Apr 15–Oct 14, 9–5:30 daily;
Oct 15–Apr 14, 9–4:30 daily

All ages

and Sunday Wave Hill holds an art workshop open to children of all ages. The workshops begin with an outdoor activity (in warmer months), giving children a chance to observe the natural world with the help of the artist leader. They then go indoors to a large craft room where they'll leisurely make that day's project.

Even without the workshops, there's plenty to entice both parents and families. To school-age children, Wave Hill is a secret garden where they can look for fairies and butterflies; a castle where they can be royalty; a fortress where they can protect their loyal subjects; or an enchanted forest where they can play hide-and-seek.

If you like this sight, you may also like the New York Botanical Garden (#27).

KEEP IN MIND Getting here without a car is simple. Wave Hill provides free shuttles to pick people up at the 242nd Street subway stop (on the 1 line), and Metro North (Riverdale station). Generally these run hourly, but check their Web site for the latest details, as they can change seasonally. It is an easy five-minute walk from the Henry Hudson Parkway/252nd Street bus stop, where numerous express buses drop off passengers. Bx7, Bx10, BxM1, and BxM2 all stop there.

YANKEE STADIUM

The House that Ruth Built is now in pieces all over the world. After the stadium was torn down, pieces of the "rubble," such as the blue seats, were sold off to collectors. The new, completely modern arena bears little resemblance to the old, with upscale restaurants (by stadium standards), luxury suites, and premium seating. But the spirit of fans rooting for the home team made the move from old stadium to new.

The best way to experience the stadium is, of course, to go to a game there. The park opens two hours before each game, and kids can often score an autograph from a player before the end of batting practice if they move close to the field. Before the game, walk around Monument Park, which contains plaques and memorials to the all-time greats: Mickey Mantle, Joe DiMaggio, Lou Gehrig, and the Babe, as well as a tribute plaque remembering September 11.

MAKE THE MOST OF YOUR TIME

Consider all your travel options: the subway is the cheaper option at $2.25 a ride, but the trip takes about 45 minutes. By contrast, taking Metro North out of Grand Central takes 13 minutes but can cost $13 (peak hours).

EATS FOR KIDS One distinct improvement in the new Yankee Stadium is the food offerings. Forget having only old hot dogs and stale Cracker Jacks. Now there are several sit-down offerings, including Hard Rock Cafe and NYY Steak. There's an entire range of quick-serve foods from popular local and national brands, including Melissa's for fresh fruit and salads, Brother Jimmy's BBQ, and Popcorn Indiana, and for parents, Beers of the World.

 1 E. 161st St., Bronx

718/293-4300;
www.newyorkyankees.com

 Games $14 and up; tours
$15–$25 ages 15 and up,
$8–$15 children 14 and under

 Tours M–Sa 9–4:40 except
when team plays at home

5 and up

Tickets are easier to come by now that there's more room in the stadium. Still, planning in advance is always a good idea, especially for popular games. And unless you are ready to pay top dollar, forget Subway Series seats (aka when the Yankees and the Mets face off).

Take the tour if you can't make the game. The Classic Tour lasts an hour and goes three places: New York Yankees Museum, Monument Park, and the Yankees dugout.

You can also opt for tickets to the city's two minor-league teams, the Brooklyn Cyclones and Staten Island Yankees. These often delight kids more than the major leagues, with the action so close and fun events just for kids (see Coney Island #52).

If you like this site, you may also like Madison Square Garden (#37).

KEEP IN MIND The crowds in the stadium interior can be intense, so guest services provides wristbands to help children identify their seat locations; look for the Tag-A-Kid guest services booths throughout the stadium to get a wristband. Also, check the Yankees Web site to take note of games where promotions or giveaways are scheduled: caps, stuffed toys, and trading cards are among the items given out, sometimes only to kids 12 and under (which will make them feel particularly special).

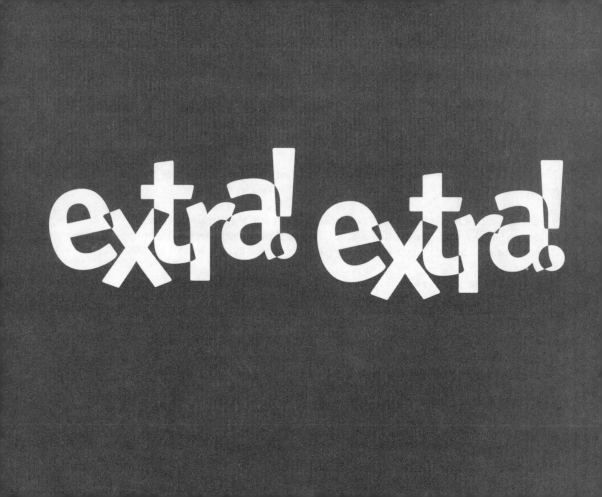

CLASSIC GAMES

"I SEE SOMETHING YOU DON'T SEE AND IT IS BLUE." Stuck for a way to get your youngsters to settle down in a museum? Sit them down on a bench in the middle of a room and play this vintage favorite. The leader gives just one clue—the color—and everybody guesses away.

"I'M GOING TO THE GROCERY STORE..." The first player begins, "I'm going to the grocery store and I'm going to buy . . ." and finishes the sentence with the name of an object, found in grocery stores, that begins with the letter "A." The second player repeats what the first player has said, and adds the name of another item that starts with "B." The third player repeats everything that has been said so far and adds something that begins with "C," and so on through the alphabet. Anyone who skips or misremembers an item is out (or decide up front that you'll give hints to all who need 'em). You can modify the theme depending on where you're going that day, as "I'm going to X and I'm going to see . . ."

FAMILY ARK Noah had his ark—here's your chance to build your own. It's easy: Just start naming animals and work your way through the alphabet, from antelope to zebra.

PLAY WHILE YOU WAIT

NOT THE GOOFY GAME Have one child name a category. (Some ideas: first names, last names, animals, countries, friends, feelings, foods, hot or cold things, clothing.) Then take turns naming things that fall into that category. You're out if you name something that doesn't belong in the category—or if you can't think of another item to name. When only one person remains, start again. Choose categories depending on where you're going or where you've been— historic topics if you've seen a historic sight, animal topics before or after the zoo, upside-down things if you've been to the circus, and so on. Make the game harder by choosing category items in A-B-C order.

DRUTHERS How do your kids really feel about things? Just ask. "Would you rather eat worms or hamburgers? Hamburgers or candy?" Choose serious and silly topics—and have fun!

BUILD A STORY "Once upon a time there lived . . ." Finish the sentence and ask the rest of your family, one at a time, to add another sentence or two. If you can, record the narrative— and you can enjoy your creation again and again.

GOOD TIMES GALORE

WIGGLE & GIGGLE Give your kids a chance to stick out their tongues at you. Start by making a face, then have the next person imitate you and add a gesture of his own—snapping fingers, winking, clapping, sneezing, or the like. The next person mimics the first two and adds a third gesture, and so on.

JUNIOR OPERA During a designated period of time, have your kids sing everything they want to say.

THE QUIET GAME Need a good giggle—or a moment of calm to figure out your route? The driver sets a time limit and everybody must be silent. The last person to make a sound wins.

BEST BETS

BEST IN TOWN
American Museum of Natural History
Bronx Zoo
Central Park
Coney Island
New York Hall of Science

BEST OUTDOORS
Brooklyn Bridge and DUMBO
Bronx Zoo
Central Park
Coney Island
Victorian Gardens

BEST CULTURAL ACTIVITY
Broadway on a Budget
Guggenheim
New Victory Theater
Rubin Museum
Symphony Space

BEST MUSEUM

American Museum of Natural History

Brooklyn Children's Museum

Guggenheim

Metropolitan Museum of Art

New York Historical Society

WACKIEST

Coney Island

F.A.O. Schwarz

Madame Tussauds Wax Museum

Moomah

Sony Wonder Technology Lab

SOMETHING FOR EVERYONE

ART ATTACK
Brooklyn Museum **59**
Children's Museum of the Arts **53**
El Museo del Barrio **51**
Guggenheim **45**
Jewish Museum **42**
Metropolitan Museum of Art **36**
Museum of Modern Art **33**
National Museum of the American Indian **31**
Noguchi Museum & Socrates Sculpture Garden **20**
Rubin Museum **12**

COOL 'HOODS
Books of Wonder/Cupcake Cafe **65**
Brooklyn Bridge and DUMBO **61**
Lower East Side Tenement Museum **39**
Moomah **35**
Prospect Park **19**
South Street Seaport Museum **9**

FREEBIES
Alley Pond Environmental Center **68**
The Cathedral Church of St. John the Divine **58**
National Museum of the American Indian **31**
New York Public Library **22**
Queens Museum **16**
Sony Wonder Technology Lab **10**

GAMES AND AMUSEMENTS
Coney Island **52**
F.A.O. Schwarz **48**
Toys"R"Us **5**
Victorian Gardens **3**

GOOD SPORTS/ PHYSICAL FUN
Chelsea Piers **55**
Greenway Bike/Walking Path **46**
Karma Kids Yoga **41**
Madison Square Garden **37**
Rockefeller Center and the Ice Rink **13**
Yankee Stadium **1**

ALL AROUND TOWN

BATTERY PARK
Greenway Bike/Walking Path **46**
National Museum of the American Indian **31**

BRONX
Bronx Zoo **63**
New York Botanical Garden **27**
Wave Hill **2**
Yankee Stadium **1**

BROOKLYN
Brooklyn Botanic Garden **62**
Brooklyn Bridge and DUMBO **61**
Brooklyn Children's Museum **60**
Brooklyn Museum **59**
Coney Island **52**
New York Aquarium **28**
New York Transit Museum **21**
Prospect Park **19**
Prospect Park Zoo **18**
Puppetworks **17**

CENTRAL PARK
Central Park **57**
Central Park Zoo **56**
F.A.O. Schwarz **48**
Victorian Gardens **3**

LOWER EAST SIDE
Lower East Side Tenement
Museum **39**

MIDTOWN
Empire State Building **49**
Intrepid Sea, Air & Space Museum **43**
Madison Square Garden **37**
Museum of Modern Art **33**
New York Public Library (main branch) **22**
Sony Wonder Technology Lab **10**
United Nations **4**

MANY THANKS

The first thanks goes to *kidcityny.com* members who have generously shared their time and family city secrets with us over the years and the children who patiently ventured forth with me to the good, the bad, and the ugly, especially Sierra, Georgia, Olivia, Katie, Grace, Paloma, and Emilia. Next to the people who supported us emotionally, financially, logistically, and in whatever other way is possible: Sara Chwatt, Fred Chapnick, Marianne Holstrom, Lynn Rigney and Larry Saul, Linda Corradina, Vicki and Ed Rich, Jennifer Essen, and Ciaran O'Reiley.

To the bold, creative, fun, lighthouse of inspiration Maria Hart, who let me call although she'd prefer e-mail. Partner is a better title for you than Editor. To the other Superwoman editor, Laura Kidder, who saw something in me that set my life on a totally different course and to whom I shall be forever grateful.

To the PR professionals who endure heated rejection and hang-ups from journalists all day long but still share their smiles and suggestions with us when we call, especially Katie Laucks, Melissa Cantor, Sara Joseph, Alanna Schindewolf, Lowell Eschen, Chas Stovall, Didi Lutz, Laura Davidson, Jennifer Hawkins, Katie Chapman, and Louise O'Brien. (Apologies for anyone I missed). And finally, to Bamdrew (Jimm Meloy) who walked in the room with such elegant hands and that sexy Scottish accent. Thanks for spending the past 10 years casting off the bowlines and sailing away from the safe harbor with me.

—Samantha Chapnick